The CAMBRIDGESHIRE COOKBOOK
Second Helpings

A celebration of the amazing food & drink on our doorstep.
Featuring over 50 stunning recipes.

The Cambridgeshire Cookbook:
Second Helpings

©2018 Meze Publishing Ltd. All rights reserved.

First edition printed in 2018 in the UK.

ISBN: 978-1-910863-33-6

Thank you to: Mark Abbott, Midsummer House

Compiled by: Anna Tebble, Gavin McArthur

*Written by: Katie Fisher, Alana Bishop,
Ella Michele, Muirne Cunning*

*Photography by: Tim Green
www.timgreenphotographer.co.uk*

Edited by: Phil Turner

Designed by: Matt Crowder, Paul Cocker

PR: Hannah Keith

*Contributors: Faye Bailey, Sarah Koriba,
David Wilson, Rachel Havard, Zofia Filipowicz*

Cover art: Luke Prest (www.lukeprest.com)

Published by Meze Publishing Limited
Unit 1b, 2 Kelham Square
Kelham Riverside
Sheffield S3 8SD
Web: www.mezepublishing.co.uk
Telephone: 0114 275 7709
Email: info@mezepublishing.co.uk

Printed by Bell & Bain Ltd, Glasgow

FOREWORD

When I first moved down to Cambridge, I knew it was a lovely city, with historic buildings and world-renowned colleges and universities, but that was all I knew about Cambridge.

I joined the Midsummer House team back in 2010. Prior to this I had worked at Deans in Belfast, Restaurant Andrew Fairlie and 21212 in Edinburgh.

As with all new jobs, you throw yourself in and give 110%. It took me almost a year to really start to appreciate what Cambridge had to offer. Of course, I'm now thankful to the area for all its outstanding produce.

It's so exciting for a chef when a new local producer or supplier comes into the kitchen with fantastic ingredients. Our asparagus, and many of the fruit and vegetables that we use, are grown less than ten miles away from the restaurant. We have a cheese company that works tirelessly alongside us, discovering new and exciting gems that this county has to offer. The variety of independent restaurants who are serving fantastic food here are in abundance too, amidst beautiful scenery.

Midsummer sits on the banks of the picturesque River Cam, opposite Cambridge's famous rowing clubs and also over looks Midsummer Common, so on an almost daily basis we can have the herd of cows who live on the common standing on the pathway waiting to greet our guests. I'm sure you'll agree that there are not many restaurants out there that can boast this!

Midsummer is a restaurant that never stands still. It is constantly evolving and changing for the better. It's a very exciting place to be part of. No day is ever the same and we all work together as a team to give our guests the very best dining experience that we can.

I really hope that you enjoy the book. I feel with the vast amount and variety of restaurants Cambridgeshire has to offer, there is definitely something for everyone.

Mark Abbott – Head chef, Midsummer House

CONTENTS

Anchors AWAY

The Anchor has been in the capable hands of Benjamin Crick and Jean-Mary Myers for just over a year, and has undergone a welcome and impressive transformation during that time...

Having been a chef for more than 20 years, Ben Crick has realised a long-held ambition of running his own place and cooking his own food at The Anchor in the Cambridgeshire village of Burwell. Built in 1760, the charming Grade II listed Georgian building was in need of loving care and attention and he and Jean-Mary have given it just that. The couple have restored and refurbished it themselves to create a wonderful destination, complete with a restaurant, snug and bar.

A warm homely welcome greets customers with cosy sofas, re-upholstered chairs and blinds made by Jean-Mary, a well-stocked bar of craft gins and beers or choice of loose leaf teas served in colourful super-size mugs. There are also board games, a record player, a craft box with knitting and crochet to enjoy as well as a friendly nuzzle from their collie, Bluebell.

The superb food and friendly, professional service has already earned The Anchor an enviable reputation. Everything is cooked to order from Ben's menu, which changes weekly as he makes the most of quality seasonal produce. "I'm so lucky to have fantastic suppliers in the area and be able to source the very best meat, fish, fruit and veg," the chef says. His modern British dishes are simple and fresh, revealing his expertise and understanding of flavour combinations.

Inspiring dishes on the evening menus include wild mushroom and tarragon risotto, seared sea bream with squid and spinach sofrito, 35-day aged ribeye with blue cheese fondue, lemon and lime posset, and the salted caramel doughnuts which are to die for! On Sundays traditional roast dinners with all the trimmings take centre stage with prime cuts of aged sirloin, pork loin and meltingly soft lamb shanks. It's the kind of food that he and Jean-Mary love and want to share.

The Anchor has been a labour of love for the determined pair; managing every aspect of the business is a new challenge for them and their small team. There's more sprucing up and knuckling down ahead, but Ben and Jean-Mary are in it together with the most important advantage at their disposal: a real passion for doing something well and plenty of well-deserved pride taken in the way they do it.

The Anchor
HAM HOCK TORTELLINI AND PEA VELOUTÉ

Pea and ham have always been two ingredients that work well together in terms of flavour and texture. Ben remembers the smell of pea and ham soup cooking from his mum's kitchen when coming home from school; this recipe is his version of pea and ham soup with an interesting twist.

Preparation time: 30 minutes, plus overnight and 1 hour resting
Cooking time: 2 hours 40 minutes | Makes 12 large tortellini

Ingredients

For the ham hock:

600g ham hock

1 carrot

1 onion, halved

12 peppercorns

For the pasta:

600g 00 pasta flour

7 large eggs

Sprinkle of semolina

For the chicken mousse:

1 skinless chicken breast

2 egg whites

400ml cream

For the pea velouté:

1 litre fresh ham stock

500g frozen peas

To serve:

Handful of pea shoots

2 tbsp Parmesan shavings

Method

For the ham hock

The ham hock will need to have been soaked in cold water in the fridge overnight. Drain the water off, cover the hock with fresh water, add the carrot, the halved onion, the peppercorns and bring to the boil. Then, turn down to a simmer and slow cook for 2 to 2 and a half hours until tender. Afterwards, leave the hock to cool in the stock. Once cool enough to touch, carefully remove the hock into a colander with a bowl underneath to catch the drips and pull apart the meat, throwing the bones, sinew and fat away. Reserve the meat and keep one litre of stock for the velouté. Set a small handful of ham hock aside for garnish; the rest will be used in the chicken mousse.

For the pasta

To make the pasta, blend the flour and six eggs in a food processor until they resemble breadcrumbs. Then, on a floured surface, knead together the breadcrumb-like mixture until it forms a dough. Shape into a ball, wrap in cling film and place in the fridge for 30 minutes.

To make the tortellini, roll the dough through a pasta machine on the thinnest setting. Then, on a floured surface, cut the pasta into 12 circles using a 10cm diameter round cutter and add a teaspoon of chicken mousse into the centre of the pasta circles. Next, beat the remaining egg and brush the egg wash over one side of the pasta around the mousse. Fold over the pasta to form a semi-circle and with the outside arch of your thumb, press the pasta down along all the edge until all the air has squeezed out and the pasta has sealed together. Bring round the two ends and pinch together to form the tortellini and place onto a tray lined with baking parchment and a sprinkling of semolina (this is to stop the pasta sticking to the bottom).

For the chicken mousse

To make the chicken mousse, dice the chicken breast and place in a food processor. Blitz to a paste, and then add the two egg whites and give a 5 second pulse to bind it together then slowly pour the double cream into the mixer while blending on a low speed until required consistency. Transfer into a bowl, add the pulled ham hock and mix together. Cover and refrigerate.

For the velouté

To make the pea velouté, use a saucepan to bring the litre of ham stock to a boil, add the frozen peas and then bring back to the boil. Use a slotted spoon to remove a handful of peas at this point for garnish. Using a stick blender, purée the ham stock with the remaining peas into a velouté.

To serve

In a large pan of lightly salted boiling water, place the tortellini in and simmer for five minutes. Drain and serve the tortellini in a bowl, pour the pea velouté around it and garnish with ham pieces, peas, peashoots and Parmesan shavings.

From East to WEST

Jin Yee Chung is a baker who brings the unique flavours and textures of south-east Asia to the UK, through the desserts he creates in his Cambridge kitchen...

The beginning of The Baking Jin's story goes right back to Jin Yee Chung's childhood in Borneo, Malaysia. His mum, an exceptional baker who baked commercially and gave baking classes, provided the inspiration that played a crucial part in his eventual return to baking. "I was a lazy kid though; I watched her bake a lot but I never baked with her!" says Jin. Years later, when a friend persuaded him to enter the Cambridge Bake Off he used the flavours and textures from his childhood home in the final round, winning the competition. A guest appearance in the first Cambridgeshire Cook Book followed and established a foundation for his new venture: The Baking Jin.

Since then, Jin has been very busy baking. His business relies on word of mouth and social media for promotion, as well as the great support of local foodies. From small beginnings and what Jin describes as "a happy accident", The Baking Jin is becoming well known, especially for the trademark chiffon cake. This is a very light and soft cake, not overly sweet and combined with exotic flavours, such as pandan and black sesame; it's now regularly available from a local café. In Jin's kitchen, it's not unusual to find cakes flavoured with tropical fruits and oriental ingredients alongside old favourites like strawberries and cream; a true fusion of East and West. Sourcing the best ingredients can be challenging, and many of Jin's bakes require ingredients which are hard to find in the UK, so he makes frequent trips to importers in London and international markets.

The Baking Jin is a 'one man band' presently run entirely from his home kitchen. What makes it so special is Jin's passion to create something unique. "It is so rewarding when people enjoy the whole experience, from the visual appeal to the flavour and textures," says Jin. He currently accepts cake commissions for special celebrations, parties, and local cafés. He also does pop-ups, collaborations, and cakes for people who just want to experience something delicious, and not available elsewhere.

"I want people to come to The Baking Jin to taste something different - something completely out of the ordinary."

The Baking Jin
MANGO POMELO SAGO CAKE ROLL

Mango pomelo sago is a classic dessert in the Far East. I have reconstructed
this recipe by incorporating a very light sponge combined with the mango
pomelo sago dessert ingredients to make a cake roll. Serving people with sweet
treats makes them happy, which makes me happy, too!

Preparation time: 45 minutes, plus 4 hours chilling | Cooking time: approx. 40 minutes | Serves 8-10

Ingredients

¼ pomelo (3 to 4 segments)

2 ripe mangoes, chopped into 1cm cubes

30g sugar

½ tsp lemon juice

For the sponge:

4 eggs, separated into yolks and whites

60g sunflower oil

30ml water

60g flour

Pinch of salt

50g sugar

For the filling:

30g sago (fine tapioca pearl)

300ml water

1 pandan leaf (optional)

300g double cream

40g icing sugar

Method

First, take the pomelo segments, remove the white pith and separate some of the juicy cells. Put 150g of the cubed mango, 30g of sugar and lemon juice in a blender, and blend into a fine purée.

For the sponge

Preheat the oven to 165°c. Grease a 25x30cm shallow baking tray and line the base and sides with one piece of baking parchment. Place the egg yolks, sunflower oil, water and 30g of mango purée in the bowl. Whisk by hand until combined. Sift in the flour and salt, then mix again until combined.

In a separate clean bowl, beat the egg whites with an electric mixer until they form soft peaks, add half the sugar and continue to beat for 15 seconds, then add the remaining sugar, and continue to beat until it forms stiff peaks. Gently fold the egg whites into the egg yolk mixture, until they are well combined with no streaks of egg whites visible.

Pour into the prepared baking tray, and bake for 22 minutes. Remove from the oven, gently peel off the baking paper, and let the sponge cool down. In the meantime, prepare the filling.

For the filling

Add the sago and water to a saucepan. You can also add a pandan leaf tied into a knot to the pan which will impart a slight fragrance. Simmer over a medium heat for 15 minutes or until the sago turns transparent. Over the sink, pour the sago into a fine sieve, run cold water from tap over it to wash away the sticky starch, discard the pandan leaf and then set aside. In a clean bowl, whip double cream, icing sugar and 30g of mango purée until the mixture is firm and forms trails. Fold the sago into the mango cream.

To assemble

Cut a piece of parchment paper so you have 10cm extra on each side of the sponge. When the sponge is completely cool, place on the paper and spread the prepared filling evenly over the top. Lay fresh mango cubes and pomelo cells in a row across the middle of the long side and drizzle the remaining mango purée on top. Gently but decisively roll the sponge over. Once you roll up the sponge, secure the roll by twisting the parchment paper at both ends. Refrigerate for at least 4 hours to firm up the cream. Unwrap the roll, slice off 1cm from each end and decorate to your preference. Slice and serve. Keep refrigerated, if it doesn't get eaten straight away!

Clay Cooking
REVOLUTION

Balkan Pottery offers even more than its name suggests; the range of rustic earthenware is robust enough to be used for cooking as well as beautiful when used for serving food and drink – a game-changer for dinner parties and al fresco eating!

Felicity Mclachlan came across an opportunity to bring something very unique to the UK during one of her visits to Bulgaria, where she travels to regularly with her partner Barry. The spark was lit when she was served with a beautiful wine decanter in a restaurant and asked about the origins of the pottery. It took some detective work to find the maker, but when Barry tracked them down, Felicity bought her first amphora and a chicken cooker, which is the only piece of kitchenware she's used to cook a chicken on since! She began importing the handmade pieces from the suppliers in Bulgaria – all small family-run businesses – which have been such a hit that running Balkan Pottery is now her full-time job.

The venture has taken Felicity to shows, farmers' markets and food festivals across the country and she also has a website set up with an online shop. Although she's not a chef Felicity has come up with lots of fun, simple but really tasty ideas for cooking with the clay kitchenware in her range. It includes the now renowned chicken cooker, which is specially designed to make cooking a perfect roast dinner almost fuss-free every

time. The dish has a funnel in the centre on which the chicken sits upright, allowing the skin to get crispy all over while the veg cook in the base below. The really clever part is the steam created inside the bird from the liquid you can fill the funnel with – wine, beer, coca cola, all infuse the meat with lots of flavour as well as keeping it really juicy.

Balkan Pottery cooking is more versatile than just roast chicken, though it's a great place to start. The funnel dish can be used with all sorts of other meats and has even been used with a whole cauliflower. Other popular items include a Sach dish, that comes with a holder so the food can go straight to the table, the amphora, pie dishes, casseroles and crockery too. Clay is a fantastic conductor, Felicity explains, so it retains the heat and cooks really evenly while looking rather beautiful in front of your guests!

Balkan Pottery products encourage communal eating, cooking without stress for the host, and having reliable recipes to enjoy when the occasion strikes – everything Felicity and Barry love about cooking for friends and family.

Balkan Pottery
ROAST CHICKEN WITH A TWIST

You can use this recipe as more of a guideline to creating amazing roast dinners with whatever size of chicken cooker suits you and your family or friends. Swap out the root vegetables, serve the whole pot straight from the oven or use the juices in the base to make a really flavourful sauce, experiment with different liquids in the funnel such as wine, beer or cola – the choice is yours. This style of cooking is designed to be simple and fun but always produces great results, with minimal input from the host!

Preparation time: 30 minutes | Cooking time: 2 hours | Serves 4

Ingredients

Roasting potatoes, peeled and chopped

Parsnips, peeled and chopped

Carrots, peeled and chopped

3 or 4 red onions, peeled and sliced

4 cloves of garlic, peeled and sliced

Olive oil and salt

Cranberry juice

1 large chicken

2 tsp soy sauce

2 tsp brown sugar

For the gravy:

100ml red wine

2-3 tsp cranberry sauce

Method

First, parboil the potatoes, parsnips and carrots for 10 minutes. Meanwhile, layer the sliced onion and garlic in the base of the chicken cooker. Drain the vegetables in a colander and shake to rough up the edges. Put in a bowl and mix with a little oil and salt, then arrange them into the dish on top of the onion. Pour the cranberry juice into the funnel of the chicken cooker until half to three quarters full and then place the chicken - bottom first - over the top so it stands up but rests on the vegetables. Unhook the wings so they sit in front. Mix the soy sauce and brown sugar together in a small bowl and then brush the mixture over the whole chicken.

Put the chicken cooker in the oven and set the temperature to 180°c (200°c if not a fan oven). Cook for 1-1½ hours until the juices run clear when the chicken skin is pierced. Cooking the chicken is not particularly time specific though, as the meat won't dry out and you don't have to baste or even check it during this time. You may wish to turn the vegetables over halfway through cooking, but leave the onion in the base to soak up all the juices.

For the gravy

Take the chicken off the cooker to rest once done. Take the potatoes and other root vegetables out of the base and spoon the onion, garlic and juices into a jug. Replace the vegetables and put the cooker back in the oven to keep everything warm. Using a hand blender, blend the gravy base and then transfer it into a small pan. Add the red wine and cranberry sauce and heat till simmering.

To serve

Put the chicken back onto the funnel and carve the meat on the dish at the table. Serve with some steamed green vegetables or a side of your choice

Good INTENTS

Bedouin and Al Casbah are family-run Algerian restaurants that bring all the warmth and flavour of North Africa and the Mediterranean to Cambridge.

With two restaurants and a new catering business to their name, Karim and his family aren't short on know-how and even more importantly, they share a passion for bringing authentic North African cuisine to Cambridge. The one that started it all, Al Casbah, recently began its 20th year with a sense of regeneration in the air. When father of five Foudil established the restaurant he brought the flavours and atmosphere of his home country, Algeria, to the heart of his venture, and that sense of authenticity and feeling of welcome has been retained through all the changes it's seen. The tented ceiling and decorative touches create a colourful and relaxed interior, designed to marry beautifully with the street food vibe. Marinated meat and vegetables, freshly prepared mezze – including homemade hummus, tabbouleh and baba ganoush – and a choice of accompaniments comprise an interactive menu, cooked on a magnificent charcoal grill right in front of the customers.

This fresh take on classic Algerian food was developed through a collaborative approach. Foudil's eldest son Karim learnt the ropes at an early age alongside his four younger brothers – earning their pocket money by helping out in the restaurant at weekends – and took over the management, before moving on to open their next restaurant, leaving Yacine in charge at Al Casbah. Bedouin focuses on the comforting home-style cooking found across Algeria and aims to transport diners to the desert sands under its real Saharan tent. From Moroccan furniture to hand-painted Tunisian crockery, the experience of eating and drinking at Bedouin is the real deal. A wide range of tagines are some of the most popular menu choices, and both restaurants have plenty of options whether guests eat meat or not. Having developed the menu and set the restaurant on its current path, Karim then handed the reins to his brothers Djamel and Nacer.

Full of ambition, Karim has now branched out into events catering and brought the hub of all three businesses under one roof. Bedouin Caterers can provide everything from heaped plates of freshly cooked North African fare to candles and crockery to set the mood. Private dining for groups can include waiter service and a personalised meal, and weddings or parties for any occasion looking for bespoke and memorable catering need look no further. Karim also plans to secure a spot in Cambridge Market, as well as running Arabic food workshops to teach others about the wonderful cuisine so integral to his family… watch this space!

Bedouin BASTILLA

A typical Moroccan delicacy, bastilla is an explosion of sweet and savoury flavour and by far the most popular starter on our menu. The moist filling enclosed in crisp pastry with crunchy almonds gives it a real wow factor, so don't let the "weird combination" scare you: chicken and icing sugar really does work!

Preparation time: 30-40 minutes | Cooking time: 5 minutes | Makes 9-10

Ingredients

4 tbsp ground turmeric

2 cinnamon sticks

Salt and pepper

3 chicken breasts (you can use legs, thighs, or a combination instead)

3 large onions

2 tbsp ghee or vegetable oil and butter

4 tbsp granulated sugar

2 tbsp ground ginger

1 bunch of coriander, chopped

100g flaked almonds, toasted

Brik pastry (1 packet of 10 sheets)

1 egg white

200-300ml cooking oil

Icing sugar and ground cinnamon, to dust

Method

Bring a pan of water to the boil and add half of the turmeric, one cinnamon stick, and some salt and pepper. Add the chicken and poach for 15-20 minutes. Do not over boil as the chicken will become dry.

Meanwhile peel, halve and slice the onions fairly thinly. Heat the ghee in a large frying pan, and then add the onions with the other cinnamon stick and granulated sugar. Season and then caramelise the onion until brown. Add the ginger and remaining turmeric. Mix well.

Evenly distribute the almonds in a baking tray and then put in the oven at 180°c for 5-10 minutes. Keep a close eye on them and occasionally shake the tray so they toast evenly. Set aside.

Once the chicken is cooked through, remove it from the water, leave to cool and then cut into small pieces (if using chicken legs pick the meat off the bone with your fingers, though it's best to use gloves as the turmeric can stain!). Mix the chicken with the onion, toasted almonds and chopped coriander. Taste the filling for seasoning and if a little dry add another spoonful of ghee.

Lay out a sheet of brik pastry and fold the sides into the middle to make a rectangle. Place 50-70g of the mixture at the base and fold the bottom left corner over to the right side to make a triangle, then fold from right to left, repeating until you reach the top of the pastry sheet. Leave a bit of pastry at the top, brush with egg white and close the parcel.

Fill a saucepan to about 3-4 cm with oil and leave it on a medium heat for 5 minutes. Dip a corner of pastry into the oil to check the temperature – if the oil is not hot enough the pastry will absorb the oil and if it is too hot it will burn – and adjust the heat accordingly. Fry the bastilla on both sides for a couple of minutes, until golden brown. Carefully remove once done and drain on kitchen paper to absorb excess oil.

To serve

Arrange the bastilla on a board and dust with icing sugar. Criss cross with cinnamon, garnish with more almonds and coriander and serve with a mixed leaf salad.

Al Casbah
COUSCOUS ROYALE

For this traditional Algerian recipe, ideally use a couscoussier but you can improvise using a stock pot with a small-holed colander on top. This must fit snugly to avoid loss of vapour, so that the couscous becomes lovely and fluffy and the meat stays moist. This dish is all about timing and the balance of flavours.

Preparation time: 30 minutes | Cooking time: 1 hour 30 minutes | Serves 4

Ingredients

500g lamb, cut into 4 pieces (shoulder or leg work well)

Splash of vegetable oil

2 onions, grated

1 tbsp ground turmeric

1 tbsp paprika

1 tbsp ground ginger

1 tbsp ras el hanout (North African mixed spice)

2 cinnamon sticks

Salt and pepper

4-6 tomatoes, peeled and deseeded

2 tbsp tomato purée

4 chicken drumsticks or thighs

4 carrots

3 turnips

3 courgettes

2 sticks of celery

500g couscous

50g butter or ghee

1 tin of chickpeas

4 merguez sausages (spicy Algerian sausage)

1 tsp cinnamon powder, to garnish

1 tbsp chopped parsley, to garnish

Method

Brown the lamb on a low heat with a touch of oil for a few minutes. Add the onion, fry till golden (about 10 minutes) and then add the turmeric, paprika, ginger, ras el hanout, cinnamon sticks and salt and pepper. Stir well. Add the tomatoes and tomato purée with 1.7 litres of hot water and cook for 20-30 minutes. Add the chicken and cook for a further 30 minutes. Meanwhile, peel the carrots and cut lengthways, peel the turnips and cut into quarters, cut the courgettes into chunks, cut celery into 5cm pieces. Add the celery, turnips and carrots to cook for 15 minutes. Meanwhile, add a little oil and salt to the raw couscous grain in a bowl and mix well, then wet with 570ml warm water. Use your fingers or a fork to open up the grain by fluffing it gently. Once the grain has absorbed the water, transfer it to the couscoussier or colander and place on top of the stock pot. Allow 10 minutes for it to steam. Add the courgette chunks. Put the couscous back into the bowl, fluff up with a fork and add a small glass of cold water. Repeat the steaming process for 5-10 minutes. When the couscous is cooked, fluff up again in the bowl and add the butter or ghee. By this time all the veg and meat should be cooked. Remove from the sauce and set aside. Add the chickpeas, taste for salt (add a little more ras el hanout if required) and then boil for 10 minutes. The sauce should be fairly thin but full of flavour. Fry or grill merguez sausages, set aside.

To serve

Take four bowls, half fill each with couscous, place some vegetables on top, sprinkle over a pinch of cinnamon powder, and then add 1 piece of lamb, chicken and sausage. Ladle the sauce with the chickpeas in over and top with fresh parsley. Goes brilliantly with harissa for a bit of a kick!

Brunch with BOHEMIA

St Neots' own independent bistro serves a varied menu of breakfast, brunch and lunch dishes from around the world – with an emphasis on fresh, seasonal food and great coffee – to match the eclectic atmosphere and look of this popular feel-good place.

Bohemia is a bistro with style and substance all of its own; an industrial look crossed with bohemian vibes creates a colourful space to relax and indulge in the seasonally-inspired food and top-notch coffee. The drive behind the venture comes from James Larman and Ashley Skipp, who started out with a catering company (The Horsebox UK) whose success gave them the boost to open their own eatery. James describes the last two years of Bohemia as a lifestyle rather than a job, and one that they have absolutely loved. "It's been brilliant so far," he says, and is proud to have already scooped nominations and awards including the 2017 Best Café in Cambridgeshire from Muddy Stilettos.

Bare brick, natural wood, reclaimed and recycled materials contrast with splashes of colour to provide a warm and welcoming backdrop to the buzz of chatter throughout the day at Bohemia. Seating just under 40, the bistro kicks things off each morning with classic breakfast options alongside their signature dish "The Bohemian" – smashed avocado, smoked salmon, poached egg, and spinach on sourdough toast – and moves onto brunch and then lunch, with plenty of great

quality coffee served alongside. James and Ash like to create food from around the world with British ingredients, sourced from local suppliers as much as possible and based on the freshest seasonal availability. One wall features a chalkboard to announce the weekly-changing specials, and there are always plenty of vegetarian and vegan options so everyone finds something to love, no matter how regular their visits!

Bohemia has a great base of local custom which the lovely friendly team really support and encourage, says James. He likes people to be able to come in, make themselves comfortable, still be excited by the new dishes on offer and generally have a great time whatever the occasion. The bistro stays open for tapas evenings on Friday and Saturday nights, which have gained such a following that tables are booked up more than a month in advance! James and Ash are already planning to keep ahead of demand though, with a second premises secured for a coffee shop – diversifying but at the same time tailoring their next project to suit what people love about Bohemia – and they are excited to keep moving forwards with even more eclectic flavour and bohemian style.

Bohemia

BOHEMIA
EST 2016

Bohemia
SPANISH SCRAMBLED EGGS

Some dishes just work and this is one of those; a perfect dish to enjoy in the garden on a warm summer's morning. The hum of garlic and chilli along with the salty richness of the sumptuous scrambled egg and the crunch and chew of the chargrilled sourdough make this the ultimate breakfast.

Preparation time: 5 minutes | Cooking time: 5 minutes | Serves 2

Ingredients

12 king prawns

3 small chorizo sausages

1 clove of garlic

6 free-range eggs

2 thick slices of sourdough
(or your favourite breakfast loaf)

Fresh coriander, to taste

Large knob of butter

Drizzle of olive oil

Salt and pepper, to taste

Method

Firstly, prepare all the ingredients. Defrost the prawns or if required de-shell and de-vein them. Slice each chorizo sausage into six to eight slices, slice the red chilli, roughly chop the garlic, chop the coriander, whisk up and season the eggs and slice yourself two nice thick slices of sourdough.

Preheat the griddle pan ready for the sourdough, and put a frying pan on a medium heat. Place the chorizo into the frying pan and gently heat until the oils start to release and the chorizo starts to crisp slightly. Add the chilli and the garlic and fry gently for a few moments without allowing them to take on any colour. After about 30 seconds add the prawns and increase the heat slightly. Cook until firm and springy. Keep turning regularly to avoid anything sticking or burning and to incorporate the oils and flavours. While the prawns are cooking, drizzle some olive oil onto the sourdough and grill until lightly charred and crispy on each side.

When the prawns are cooked through add a knob of butter to the pan ready for your eggs. Put the chopped coriander into the beaten eggs and whisk again to incorporate. Quickly pour the egg mix into the pan and stir constantly into the other ingredients until the eggs are cooked to your liking.

To serve

Serve by placing the slices of sourdough toast onto a large plate and topping them with the Spanish scrambled eggs. Garnish with some more coriander and some fresh sliced chilli. Best served in the garden, with the sun shining and a steaming cup of strong coffee.

Health and HAPPINESS

Meggy and Chan's cafe is a hotspot for healthy eating in Cambridge, combining traditional Chinese cuisine with modern food that does good as well as tasting good!

During the last few years Bridges has transformed into a haven for those conscious about how they eat, as well as anyone who likes to try something a little different. They have put their heart and soul into developing the style of food they both love to eat: lots of juices, smoothies and healthy dishes, all made to order with fresh ingredients.

They have both travelled extensively and always enjoyed the opportunities this brought to try all kinds of cuisines. Having met in Hong Kong – where both Meggy and Chan are from originally – while working in a hotel, the pair still talk a lot about food and how they can bring all the influences they gleaned into their business today.

"We love learning about new combinations from many different cuisines. We really listen to our customers' needs and desires, and are constantly tweaking and modifying recipes to suit our discoveries," says Meggy. Traditional Chinese flavours and methods of cooking play a large part – many of the recipes are based on food that the couple enjoy with their families – but the emphasis is on harnessing the goodness in great produce. Where possible, the café uses local meat and organic fruit and vegetables sourced from the best local suppliers.

The food and drink on offer is designed to be simple, but tasty and fresh, and the menu is easily adaptable with lots of choice. This way, customers can eat what they want and the way they want; taking the regulars' opinions and interests into account is important at Bridges, as is updating with the times and moving with food trends. The small but busy space has recently been renovated with a bright, modern feel, catering for the needs of students, office workers and visitors. The takeaway counter and seating area are popular for breakfasts, lunches and low-sugar afternoon treats.

Bridges catering came about as a natural branch of their business and the range of options – think canapés, mini food, or perhaps a 'taste of the Orient' – is often in demand for special events or business lunches across Cambridge. Whatever your reason for visiting, Meggy and Chan offer nutritious food and refreshing juices for an eating experience that leaves you feeling great.

Bridges
CANTONESE LETTUCE WRAPS (SAN CHOY BOW)

Often promoted as a low carb dish, our recipe for lettuce wraps doesn't completely cut the carbs. Our version is balanced and can be vegetarian or not, both versions giving you the feeling of being satisfied with some carbohydrates, protein and lots of colourful vegetables. It's also quick and easy to prepare so dinner will be ready in a flash!

Preparation time: 30 minutes | Cooking time: 10 minutes | Serves 6

Ingredients

For the pork marinade:

2 tsp light soy sauce

1 tsp brown sugar

1 tbsp cornflour

2 tbsp water

For the wraps:

2 tbsp olive oil

250g pork chop or loin (not too lean), finely chopped, or firm tofu, cubed

200g glass noodles or Chinese vermicelli or cellophane noodles

4 small gem lettuces, leaves separated

1 tsp minced ginger

2 spring onions (white part only but save the green part for the garnish), finely chopped

3 cloves of garlic, minced

1 medium carrot, diced

1 stick of celery, finely chopped

1 small onion, diced

10 shiitake mushrooms (or any variety), diced

6 baby sweetcorn, diced

6 water chestnuts (fresh or canned), diced

2 tbsp yellow bean sauce

2 tsp sesame oil

For the garnish:

2 spring onions (green part), chopped

Black sesame seeds

1 lime, cut into wedges

1 fresh chilli, chopped, or chilli flakes

Method

Marinate the pork with the marinade and add a few drops of olive oil once mixed well. Let it rest for at least 20 minutes. In the meantime, soak the noodles in hot water for 10 minutes, then run under cold water. Drain and set aside. Next, trim the lettuce leaves into the shape of cups and soak in cold water for 5 minutes. Drain and set aside. Heat the remaining olive oil in a wok or pan and briefly sauté the ginger and spring onions. Add the garlic and cook for 30 seconds until fragrant then add the pork. Stir-fry for another 2 minutes.

Add the carrot, celery, onions, mushrooms and baby corn and stir-fry until all ingredients are heated through. The vegetables should still be al dente and not softened. Add the water chestnuts and noodles and finally the yellow bean sauce. Keep stir frying for approximately 2 minutes until mixed well. Turn off the heat and drizzle the sesame oil on top. Leave the mixture to cool. (If using tofu, no marinating is needed. Gently fry in a little olive oil so it stays in cubes. Add the tofu to the lettuce cups at the end, on top of the stir-fried mixture, to avoid breakage.)

To serve

Scoop the mixture into the lettuce cups and garnish with spring onions or sesame seeds. Serve with lime wedges for squeezing over, according to taste. For extra heat, serve with chopped chilli on the side. Dipping sauces are an optional way to add flavour to this already tasty dish.

Optional accompaniments

For a sweet and sour sauce mix two parts heated fish sauce, two parts rice vinegar, two parts brown sugar and one part lime juice. Add a little minced garlic and a sprinkle of chopped fresh chilli.

For a spicy peanut sauce mix three parts peanut butter, two parts soy sauce, two parts brown sugar and one part rice vinegar. Add a little minced garlic and hot chilli oil to the mixture.

The perfect fresh juice to serve with this dish is a 'Heart-Beet,' with its slightly earthy taste to complement the mildly spicy and gingery lettuce wraps. Add half a beetroot, three apples, one carrot and one stick of celery to a juicer and blend. Its a great way to make the dinner table look even more colourful, plus uses up any remaining vegetables from the food prep.

Naturally WELL-STOCKED

Burwash Larder is a modern deli and farm shop that champions local producers as well as growing asparagus and rearing rare breed pigs on the outskirts of Cambridge.

The Radford family began diversifying on their farm by selling home-grown asparagus and sweetcorn at the gate, with an honesty box for payment. Since then, they have grown the business into a thriving delicatessen and shop that are full of top-notch local fresh produce. Mike and Matt Radford work on the farm while Clare, assistant manager Tinks, and their team of food-loving locals look after the retail side of things. Burwash Larder is situated on the working organic farm, with strong links to nearby producers and suppliers. Clare says that these "good partnerships" are essential to the quality of their range, which includes over 70 British cheeses, organic veg grown on the farmland, fresh bakes and an exclusive blend of coffee from Cambridge's own Hot Numbers Coffee.

One of the main attractions at Burwash Larder is the meat from the farm's own herd of rare-breed pigs. Using old school methods and a 'quality not quantity' motto for raising and butchering the animals, the skilled team have produced sausages, ham, various cuts of pork, and bacon so good it has its own waiting list! Asparagus has its own time to shine too, during the six weeks it generally comes into season, and Burwash celebrates these fantastic products by hosting an 'Asparagus Feast' day in May and a 'Sizzling Sunday' on which barbecuing is the name of the game.

It's not just the festival-like atmosphere of these popular events that customers visit for; in fact so many of the customers are regulars that staff tend to know most by name. The purpose built oak-framed building creates a warm, natural and open feel which the team encourage through their friendly welcomes and beautiful displays of food and drink. Burwash Larder is a two-time winner of the Best Farm Shop/Deli category at the Cambridge News Food and Drink awards and is proud to be part of a community of independents on their site.

Along with producing and celebrating the best Cambridgeshire produce, the small businesses there are all committed to protecting and preserving the nature that surrounds them. Only a mile outside the city, the lakes full of dragonflies and countryside with the country's highest skylark population add something very special to the already unique experience of visiting Burwash Larder. Go for the award-winning sausages and bacon, and you'll want to stay to appreciate the feeling of a truly rural retreat just outside Cambridge, which offers a foodie day out that's far from just a shopping trip.

Burwash Larder

THE BURWASH MEATBALL SANDWICH

Our meatball subs have become a firm favourite with the lunch crowd at the deli. Made with pork from our rare breed pigs, they're a super easy way to make a deliciously filling meal. You can even make the meatball mix the night before – they're even tastier the next day and reheat easily for a quick lunch.

Preparation time: 20 minutes | Cooking time: 20 minutes | Serves 4

Ingredients

500g Burwash sausage meat (or good quality sausage meat from your local butcher)

1 onion

A knob of butter

2 cloves of garlic

1 jar (500-680g) of passata

Salt and pepper, to taste

A dash of Tabasco (if you like it hot)

100g strong farmhouse cheddar (we like Westcombe)

4 of your favourite white bread rolls or baguettes

Method

Preheat the oven to 180°c and grease a baking tray with fairly deep sides. Squeeze the sausage meat into a large mixing bowl. Use your hands to shape the mixture into 20 small meatballs, each roughly the size of a gobstopper. Place these a few centimetres apart on the greased baking tray. Put the meatballs in the oven to cook for ten minutes.

While the meatballs are cooking, slice the onion into strips around ½cm thick. Gently fry these in the butter on the hob. Finely chop the garlic and add to the onion when it has softened slightly. Fry the mixture for a few minutes until soft and on the verge of caramelising. Pour the passata over the onions and garlic and reduce the heat to a simmer. Add salt, pepper and Tabasco (if using) to taste.

When the meatballs have been in the oven for ten minutes, give them a shake and pour the sauce mixture over the top. Give everything a good mix to cover the meatballs in the sauce. Add 50ml water to thin the mixture and then pop the tray back in the oven for another 10-15 minutes to ensure the meatballs are cooked through.

While this is cooking, slice your chosen bread and grate your favourite cheese. When the meatballs are ready, place five in each sandwich along with some of the reduced sauce. Add some salad leaves if you fancy, sprinkle cheese over the top, and enjoy!

All the fun OF THE FARM

Run by a family and the perfect place to spend a family day out, Bury Lane Farm Shop is a haven for anyone who enjoys fresh seasonal produce and quality choices from hot meals to cut flowers.

The expression 'from field to fork' is never truer than when you browse the rows of pick your own strawberries, or choose a bunch of asparagus picked at the height of its brief season from Bury Lane Farm Shop. The farming family who own and work the land have grown their business into a veritable treasure trove of fresh and local produce. The farm shop incorporates a delicatessen where the focus is on offering customers something a little more unusual and special, including a range of Cambridgeshire cheeses plus cold meats, pies and quiches. It also boasts a butchers and fishmongers, featuring local and rare breed meats as well as sausages and burgers made on site, and fish straight from Billingsgate.

The emphasis on seasonal produce means everything that the team source for Bury Lane is at its freshest and best year-round. Along with asparagus and strawberries, they grow greenhouses full of flowers on the farm and also have a garden centre. The family make sure they support and engage with the fantastic range of suppliers and other producers around them in the Cambridgeshire countryside, reflecting the quality of the food and drink created in the area. The gift shop houses a range of cards, homeware, toys, jewellery and other treasures to explore. Bury Lane's longevity has made it a part of the community, and staff see customers returning time and again (sometimes surprised at how far things have developed since the venture's humble beginnings!).

Knowledgeable people who really care about what's being produced and sold are the cornerstone of Bury Lane. They always aim to provide visitors with an experience, not just a shopping trip, whether they're stocking up the fridge or just popping by to sample the scones which are well-known for being so popular. Bury Lane Bakery is also owned by the family and its deliciously fresh cakes and other treats are sold in the farm shop as well as across the county in various venues.

The choice of take-home food and drink is complemented by Bury Lane's café which comfortably accommodates crowds of people for a hot lunch or breakfast. Children can also enjoy farm-themed fun in the adjoining indoor play area. From squash to Sunday roasts, Bury Lane Farm Shop sets its sights on offering something for everyone and welcomes its visitors with plenty to explore come rain or shine.

Bury Lane Farm Shop
STRAWBERRY CHEESECAKE

Strawberry Cheesecake is always a winner, whether it's just for the family or if you have dinner guests. Our take on this classic dessert has a lovely purée topping and makes the best use of fresh, hand-picked strawberries from our farm – from field to shop with no food miles.

Preparation time: 45 minutes | Chilling time: 1 hour plus overnight | Serves 12

Ingredients

250g pack of Bury Lane Golden Oat Cookies

100g butter, melted

1 vanilla pod, split to release seeds

600g soft cheese (from our deli counter)

100g icing sugar

284ml pot double cream

For the topping:

1 punnet of Bury Lane strawberries, halved

25g icing sugar

Method

Butter and line a 23cm loose-bottomed tin with baking paper. Crush the biscuits in a plastic food bag using a rolling pin. Transfer the crumbs to a bowl, then pour over the melted butter. Mix thoroughly until the crumbs are completely coated. Tip into the prepared tin and press down firmly to create an even layer. Chill in the fridge for 1 hour to set.

Place the soft cheese, icing sugar and vanilla seeds in a bowl, then beat with an electric mixer until smooth. Tip in the cream and continue beating until combined. Spoon the cream mixture onto the biscuit base, working from the edges inwards and making sure there are no air bubbles. Smooth the top of the cheesecake down with the back of a spoon or spatula. Leave to set in the fridge overnight.

About 30 minutes before serving, bring the cheesecake to room temperature. Place the base on top of a can then gradually pull the sides of the tin down. Slip the cake onto a serving plate, remove the lining paper and base. Purée half of the strawberries in a blender or food processor with the icing sugar and 1tsp of water, and then sieve the purée. Pile the remaining strawberries onto the cake and pour over the purée to serve.

Cambridge Blue Belles WI
BELLE SOUR

The Belle Sour is the Cambridge Blue Belles WI Signature Summer Cocktail. The starting point is the idea of a cocktail sour: a balance of alcohol, sweet, sour and bitter flavours. This base always creates great cocktails and is also a good metaphor for life and the lives we lead as empowered women. We are strong (alcohol) but know we must accept the sour and bitter (lemon, cocktail bitters) along with the sweet (syrup) to lead a balanced life. Aoife, creator of the Belle Sour cocktail, just knew gin had to feature; she says there is something about the Blue Belles that makes her think of fabulous ladies drinking gin! Once that was decided, the rest of the ingredients were inspired by summer at our allotment: rhubarb, strawberries, gooseberries and lemon balm. Aoife makes her own infused syrups and spirits, but if you don't have the time or the patience for that, shop-bought cordial and vodka will do the trick.

Preparation time: 5 minutes, unless you are making your own infused spirits and syrups. You'll need to make those at least a few days in advance, but it will be worth the wait! | Serves 1

Ingredients

30ml gin

20ml rhubarb vodka

20ml strawberry, gooseberry and lemon balm syrup (we use homemade but Bottle Green make a nice range)

20ml freshly squeezed lemon juice

3-4 drops of rhubarb bitters

Method

Combine all the ingredients in a cocktail shaker, add ice and shake (or stir vigorously) for 30 seconds. Strain into glass. Garnish with a strawberry or some lemon balm leaves. Multiply as needed to make a jug full; mix all of the ingredients together and then shake each serving individually over ice. This is a good technique for party preparations.

To make an alcohol-free version of the cocktail

Replace the gin with the same quantity of apple and rhubarb juice, and the vodka with a non-alcoholic spirit (e.g. Seedlip). The rhubarb bitters are 4.5% alcohol and can be used as it's only a few drops, or omitted if you prefer. Top up with soda water to taste.

Those who dare,
GIN

From hobbyists to winners of the World Beverage Innovation Awards, husband and wife team William and Lucy are changing the face of gin.

It may be a surprise to read that the world's first gin tailor started life in a living room in Cambridge. William and Lucy Lowe, along with their faithful companion Darcy (the distillery dog) have blazed a trail of innovation which has transformed the face of the gin industry as we know it. It was while walking with Darcy in the fields around Cambridge that the couple came up with the idea of using local flora to create a gin, rather than relying on dried and imported botanicals as every other distillery did at that point.

In order to make this work, they developed a system of vacuum distillation which allowed them to distil fine and delicate botanicals at extremely low temperatures, thereby retaining elegant aromatic profiles. This allowed Master Distiller William to work with flavours previously unknown to gin production and sourced from areas as local as their own garden!

Early on, the couple realised that not everyone shares exactly the same taste in gin, and so developed a method of creating individual gins for individual people. They became the world's first gin tailor, and set about making each one of their customers their own unique concoctions. The idea caught on quickly and they soon found themselves with a waiting list over a year long, and producing gins for some of the most famous restaurants and institutions in the world, including the two-Michelin star Midsummer House, British Airways Concorde Lounge and the House of Lords. They then turned their skills to developing a unique portfolio of products including a series of world firsts (the world's first seasonal gins, first digestif gins, first gins from Japanese botanicals, to name but a few) resulting in the Cambridge Distillery being named three consecutive times as the most innovative in the world!

The distillery has recently relocated to Grantchester, and has a showroom right next door where you can stop by to sample their products, all of which have won gold medals in international competitions. In 2015 they also opened Cambridge Gin Laboratory on Green Street, which hosts daily master classes and tutored tastings as well as boasting its own interactive drinks lab dedicated to the appreciation of gin.

Despite their modest beginnings, the three founders of this unique distillery – William, Lucy, and of course Darcy – have proven that great things can come from the smallest of seeds.

The Cambridge Distillery

GIN CURED SALMON

A wonderfully light dish, ideal for a summer garden party or for entertaining.
This should be made a day ahead of time.

Preparation time: 50 minutes plus 12 hours curing | Serves 4

Ingredients

75g salt

75g caster sugar

1 tsp lime, zested

1 lime, thinly sliced (a mandoline is ideal)

½ tsp whole black peppercorns, lightly crushed

1 tsp pink peppercorns

2 tsp coriander seeds

1 tsp cumin seeds

1 tsp juniper berries, lightly crushed

80ml Cambridge Dry Gin

400g salmon fillet, skin on, pin-boned

2 cucumbers

2 tbsp mint leaves

Borage flowers, extra-virgin olive oil and toasted sourdough slices, to serve

Method

Mix together the salt, sugar, lime zest, black and pink peppercorns, spices, juniper berries and gin. Spread half of the spice mixture in a glass or ceramic dish, then add the fish, skin-side down, and cover with the remaining spice mixture. Cover with cling film and chill overnight, turning over the fish after 12 hours and spooning any liquid in the dish over the top. Remove the salmon from the dish, reserving any liquid, and rinse. Pat dry with a paper towel.

Slice the cucumbers lengthways, as thinly as possible. A mandoline or peeler is ideal for this. Marinate in the reserved liquid for 30 minutes. Drain, reserving one tablespoon of the spices from the curing liquid.

Slice the salmon on the diagonal, very thinly, discarding the skin. Arrange on a serving platter and decorate with cucumber, lime slices, mint, borage flowers and the reserved spices. Drizzle with oil and serve with fresh sourdough bread.

The Cambridge Distillery

TOKYO SNAPPER

A Japanese twist on a Red Snapper, the predecessor to the Bloody Mary.

Preparation time: 10 minutes | Serves 1

Ingredients

Lemon or lime wedge

Umami salt

50ml Japanese gin

75ml tomato juice

25ml yuzu juice

Sansho pepper or black pepper

Few drops of light soy sauce

¼ tsp wasabi powder

Cucumber ribbon to garnish

Method

Moisten the rim of a highball glass by running the wedge of lemon or lime around it. Then dip the rim into a saucer of umami salt to evenly coat. Fill with ice.

Add Japanese gin, tomato and yuzu juice to a shaker full of ice along with the pepper, soy sauce and wasabi powder. Shake until chilled, then strain into the highball glass.

Garnish with a cucumber ribbon.

The Cambridge Distillery

RIVERSIDE

Elegant and refreshing – the perfect summer cocktail.

Preparation time: 5 minutes | Serves 1

Ingredients

60ml Cambridge Dry Gin

25ml lime juice

15ml sugar syrup

8 mint leaves

Lemon verbena leaf, to garnish

Method

Add all ingredients to a shaker filled with ice, shake and then double strain into a chilled coupe glass. Garnish with lemon verbena.

Food on THE MOVE

Cambridge Food Tour offers a range of award-winning tours that take guests on a walk of discovery around Cambridge, tasting some of the best food and drink in the city along the way.

Cambridge Food Tour was set up by 'head foodie' Gerla, who wanted to turn her years of travelling experiences into a way of helping other people discover her beautiful hometown. The tours were initially designed to show visitors around Cambridge in the same way that Gerla would explore a new city: lots of walking to find the real hidden gems, with plenty of stops for a bite and a tipple every now and again! They are still the only food walking tours in the city, and the popular venture is now in its successful sixth year, employs five freelance guides to cover the range of tours available, and is always evolving to include Cambridge's newest and most exciting food and drink destinations.

It's important to Gerla, who still oversees everything as well as running some tours herself, that each experience is as personal and interactive as possible. She likes to take people off the beaten track, giving them the opportunity to see Cambridge from another perspective as well as its famous landmarks and architecture. To do this, she has built up close relationships with other businesses across the city and is constantly on the lookout for more places to stumble across. This gives the tour guides an in-depth knowledge of the local food scene, and partnerships that offer visitors a chance to sample things and try activities they could otherwise miss out on. "It's important to respect and support each other" says Gerla, about working with other Cambridge independents. The time and effort she puts in to forging and maintaining these partnerships ensures that each stop off will be of high quality and reflect the city at its best.

Any tour can be combined with an activity – a class or workshop, perhaps to make your own chocolates or try out some cocktail mixology – to make it even more fun and engaging. There are scheduled tours available six days a week, and private tours offered on request that can cater for anyone from corporate groups to birthday parties. Whether the focus is on lunch, artisan treats, gin, craft beer, or one of the many other options, the tour you pick will be designed around your requirements, especially for the private option, where the tour is really a blank slate that can take you anywhere to try anything in Cambridge!

The edibles are obviously the highlight of any tour, so the mixture of bite-sized stops to eat and drink along the way are carefully curated to offer guests a cross-section of the culinary tableau Cambridge has developed. International and local flavours make appearances in equal measure, and there is lots of street food involved. Gerla has closely followed trends and developments in the world of food and drink to keep her tours up to the minute, so now it's possible to accommodate those with dietary requirements much more easily and there's plenty of vegetarian fare incorporated too. In 2018 there will be two vegan-only tours for the first time, as part of the special edition tours that are a regular feature of the business' calendar.

Gerla's aim is for everyone on a Cambridge Food Tour to have fun, connect with other foodies, and enjoy great tastes. If her guests can do that amidst a nice atmosphere with lots of laughter and experiences to go away still talking about, then it's been a success all round. More recently, Gerla has also launched a separate business, on the same wavelength as her tours but with a more distinct approach, for those who want foodie events arranging in Cambridge. The concept of F&D Events is a completely bespoke service, building on the skills and knowledge she already has from running Cambridge Food Tour. The f is for food – as well as fun, festive and funky – and the d is for drink – as well as delicious, delightful and daring – which Gerla will bring together in a way that suits the individual family member, work colleague, or friend you want to put on an occasion to remember for.

For an insight into Cambridge's food and drink culture and the diversity that makes it such a treasure trove of culinary delights, Cambridge Food Tour and F&D Events have put themselves centre stage. It all comes back to Gerla's love of enjoying great food and drink as part of exploring somewhere new; an opportunity she now provides for visitors to a city that has so much to offer above and beyond the Cambridge most people see.

Heart of THE CITY

Cambridge Market has been running for hundreds of years in the very centre of its historic namesake. It's an ever-evolving and well-loved feature of the city with a veritable smorgasbord of fresh produce, delicious food, and local culture.

The heartbeat of a community has historically always come in the form of a traditional market, and in the city centre of Cambridge this is happily still the case today. With its location opposite the Guildhall, Cambridge Market is a hub for small businesses and people flock from all around to trade and shop here. The market includes a multitude of stalls nestled under permanent canopies, and is open seven days a week to be enjoyed in rain or shine. Warmer weather may encourage a stroll around the square, browsing and grabbing a bite to eat, but seasonal events make this a year-round destination for shoppers and visitors. Cambridge Market has won multiple awards, and is so popular that the council, who operate the market, are inundated with applications from traders hoping for the opportunity to sell here amongst the lucky hundred or so stalls currently established there.

Like at any good market, local produce is sold in abundance here. Farmers frequent the market to sell home-grown goods, resulting in a great range of fresh food to peruse at your leisure. There are fishmongers, a butcher who rears his own livestock, flavoursome fruit and veg, and tempting bakeries to name a few. As well as giving city dwellers – academics, students, professionals and families alike – the opportunity to buy really fresh food, this set-up gives people the chance to support a more environmentally friendly and sustainable system as well as the local economy.

They say never shop when you're hungry, and thankfully there's no need to at Cambridge Market! The selection of street food on offer – from snacks to hot meals – is a wonderful melting pot of cultures and cuisines. Take a trip around the world with gourmet ostrich burgers, oriental noodles, waffles, crepes, churros, sushi and sashimi, jollof rice, or a good old indulgent mac 'n cheese. "People's palates are increasingly sophisticated," says market manager Dan Ritchie, "so we make sure that our traders offer a real variety." Halloumi, barley-based stews, and burgers with alternative vegetarian fillings complete a line-up that should suit everyone.

It's not just about food either; the market celebrates the best of local culture and businesses. There are plenty of other stalls to browse; you can buy homeware, clothing, jewellery, and find a gift for every occasion. On Sundays the market is dedicated to arts and crafts, selling handmade prints, paintings, vintage treasures, and homemade gifts and trinkets. Photography from the local area is also exhibited and sold on Sundays, and there are opportunities for bike repair, which is very popular with the students! The market really celebrates the city, and values its talented residents, by showcasing some of the best Cambridge has to offer all in one place.

On top of everything else, the market also hosts a range of different events that take place throughout the year. These include seasonal events such as the Christmas market and night markets throughout the summer months. The night markets offer much of what the general market includes – delicious food and drink, produce, gifts – but they also offer the chance to enjoy the longer days and warmer evenings. Along with the night markets you can often enjoy free open air cinema screenings, which show classics and old favourites guaranteed to get people singing and dancing along! The market also hosts pop up bars, which are run by Cambridge-based independents, making it the perfect destination for an evening out in the city.

A large part of what makes Cambridge Market special is its status as a community-focused and self-motivated organisation. The success of the market is driven by the individual traders, who are committed to creating their own produce or selling others' to a high standard, which inspires loyalty in both the traders and their customers. The familiar faces lend the market a very different kind of shopping experience, which responds to the needs of its varied audience and changes as tastes and demands change. Accessible, dynamic, and very much a reflection of the city and its people, Cambridge Market is not one to be missed on your next visit!

Cambridge Market

It's Easy Being GREEN

Organic fruit and veg, sourced from local growers, packed in a box and delivered to your door: The Cambridge Organic Food Company's ethos is as simple and refreshing as the produce it distributes and the suppliers it supports.

In April 2018, The Cambridge Organic Food Company (COFCo for short) celebrated 20 years of making organic produce available to people across Cambridgeshire and beyond. It all started with Duncan Catchpole and a few college mates knocking on doors asking if people were interested in a box of organic produce…it took time to catch on, but with his dad's contacts from the family's organic apple orchard and the commitment Duncan has to living and working sustainably and ethically, the venture gradually grew into the frontrunner for organic produce it is today.

COFCo now work with almost every organic grower in the area. The boxes are fruit and veg focused, but can include bread from a local bakery, locally milled flour and other organic groceries too. Duncan's idea was to give people as much choice as they wanted, so the options range from a surprise selection – representative of the best in season across Cambridgeshire – to bespoke assortments of whatever takes your fancy. Ordering can be done online, and delivery is done by area on certain days of the week to enable their fleet of vans – half of which are now electric, charged by solar panels – to run as efficiently as possible.

Being environmentally friendly across all aspects of the business is really important to Duncan. "We live the reduce, reuse, recycle philosophy here, and it's important to our customers as well who benefit from the money we save – on reusing our delivery boxes, for example – and can shop more ethically." Fair distribution of the advantages that come with this ethos goes hand in hand with a sustainable approach; The Cambridge Organic Food Company doesn't cut any corners to value its staff, suppliers, and customers equally. For Duncan this is a huge reward in itself, and recognition like Living Wage accreditation and various awards over the years are the icing on the cake.

One particularly exciting project is on the horizon: a sustainable food hub that will reinvent the distribution process for Duncan's box scheme, but will also benefit start-ups, schools, and other local businesses with its community spaces for work and education. The future looks bright (and very green) for COFCo, as more and more people are becoming aware of ways to keep the planet healthy, all while enjoying cooking with and eating deliciously fresh food!

Cambridge Organic Food Company

Cambridge Organic Food Company
ROASTED VEGETABLE CASSEROLE

It's the blend of piquant and sweet spices that makes this hearty vegan stew so delicious. All the vegetables appear regularly in Cambridge Organic's veg boxes during the summer months, grown on local farms. As the year turns, and the contents of our veg boxes change, so you can use different combinations of vegetables depending on when you make this.

Preparation time: 20 minutes | Cooking time: 50 minutes | Serves 4

Ingredients

1 kohlrabi

1 carrot

1 green ramiro pepper

1 aubergine

4 tbsp rapeseed oil

125g mushrooms

1 onion

100g red lentils, rinsed

1 tsp ground cumin

½ tsp ground coriander

½ tsp cayenne pepper

½ tsp ginger

½ tsp cinnamon

½ tsp allspice

¼ tsp ground cloves (or four whole cloves, crushed)

½ tsp salt

400g tin of chopped tomatoes

400g Hodmedod's Carlin peas

1 tbsp spicy chutney

200g spinach

Method

Preheat the oven to 220°c. Cut the thick skin off the kohlrabi and peel the carrot. Deseed the pepper. Chop the aubergine, kohlrabi, carrot and pepper into roughly 1½cm pieces. Put them into a roasting tray and toss with three tablespoons of the rapeseed oil. Roast for thirty minutes. Roasting the vegetables not only adds flavour, but lets you get on with other things while the vegetables take care of themselves. Wipe clean and chop the mushrooms. After fifteen minutes, give the roasting vegetables a stir and add the mushrooms.

In the meantime, finely slice the onion and sweat it in the remaining rapeseed oil in a cast-iron casserole dish with a lid. Cover the lentils with water in a small saucepan and boil vigorously for ten minutes. When the onion is soft, add all the spices and salt to the casserole and then fry for a few more minutes. Add the cooked lentils (drain them first if there's still a lot of liquid). Add the chopped tomatoes and 200ml of water. Drain, rinse and add the Carlin peas to this mixture.

The roasted vegetables should now be browned and softened. Add them to the casserole, along with the spoonful of chutney. Simmer for a further twenty minutes to develop the flavours. Remove any tough stalks from the spinach. Wash and roughly chop the leaves and add to the dish a couple of minutes before serving, so they wilt but retain their vibrant green colour. Taste and adjust the seasoning if necessary.

Serve in deep bowls with warm bread or toasted pitta.

Chef's note: If you haven't come across them before, Carlin peas are small dark brown, nutty peas. They are an excellent English-grown alternative to chickpeas. Although they have been grown and eaten in this country for many centuries, most of those produced in the UK nowadays are exported to Japan, where they are still very popular. In the North East of England they are traditionally eaten on Carlin Sunday, the Sunday before Palm Sunday, while in the North West, the tradition is to eat them around Bonfire Night. Our Carlin peas are produced by Hodmedod's, an East Anglian company whose aim is to find a new market for UK-grown peas and beans. Cambridge Organic is their local distributor.

Not just an ordinary CHOCOLATIER!

Since the first Cambridgeshire Cook Book, Isabelle - owner and chocolatier at Chocolat Chocolat – has received several Great Taste awards, and not just for the handmade chocolates at her unique and well-loved Cambridge shop.

At Chocolat Chocolat, owner and chocolatier Isabelle's focus on both craftsmanship and quality ingredients produces wonderful flavour and award-winning treats, including her ice cream and hot chocolate. Isabelle is delighted to still welcome new customers regularly, as well as retaining her old customers; many still call the shop or order online after moving away to get hold of their favourites! It's now a tradition for Cambridge students (and many renowned academics) to buy one of the famous Chocolate Bouquets at the end of each term, and Isabelle also welcomes over 1000 chocolate lovers each year on her chocolate-making and tasting courses.

Isabelle started Chocolat Chocolat after living in Paris and then learning her trade in France and Belgium, with the intention of proving that great-tasting chocolate can come in many flavours and forms and doesn't have to be expensive. Judging by the feedback from Cambridge's chocolate lovers, she has done just that. Cambridge's favourite chocolate flavours are still being made in the shop kitchen, including white chocolate with strawberry, a rich dark chocolate with orange, and of course everyone's favourite: caramel, praline and sea salt. Isabelle can't stop making these favourites because so many chocolate lovers ask for them every time they visit!

By continuing to develop new flavours as well, Isabelle ensures that her range of handmade sheet chocolate is always evolving and staying in touch with changing tastes. If you're in the city centre and happen to pass the shop, you can see Isabelle or one of her chocolatiers making this famed confection, and it's even possible to taste chocolate that is only 20 minutes old. As Isabelle says, "there is something magical about chocolate that is so fresh, which allows the flavours to really bring your senses alive."

The only difficulty at Chocolat Chocolat is which treat to choose! Whether you go for a hot chocolate shot, a little pick-me-up after shopping, a treat bag of handmade sheet chocolate, or a swirl of handmade ice cream – perfect for summer days after punting on the Cam – one thing is sure… Chocolat Chocolat is definitely not just an ordinary chocolate shop.

Chocolat Chocolat
RICH CHOCOLATE MOUSSE

This is an old French family recipe handed down from my grandmother to my mother, and in turn to me, and now to my daughters...

Preparation time: 10 minutes plus 2 hours chilling time | Serves 4

Ingredients

175g dark chocolate
(55% or higher)

25g butter

3 medium eggs, white and yolk
separated

25g icing sugar

Method

Melt the chocolate with the butter in a bain-marie over a moderate heat. Separately combine the egg yolks with the icing sugar. Add the melted chocolate and butter to the mixture and stir well. Whisk the egg whites into very stiff peaks and fold carefully into the chocolate mixture. Spoon the mousse into small dessert pots or cups. Chill for at least 2 hours before serving.

To serve

If you like, decorate each pot of mousse with a whirl of crème fraîche and dark chocolate shavings, or chopped hazelnuts, and serve with a traditional French biscuit such as 'Langues de Chat' on the side.

Chocolatier's Notes

A bain-marie can be made using a saucepan with a little water in, with a glass bowl sitting on top to melt the chocolate in. The glass bowl should fit snugly on top so no water can get near the chocolate, and the water in the saucepan must not touch the bottom of the glass bowl or it could scald the chocolate. Melt the chocolate gently on a moderate heat.

Always use the freshest eggs and good quality chocolate with between 55% and 70% cocoa.

My mother often added orange zest to the mixture before folding in the egg whites, but you could also flavour the mousse with a tablespoon of strong coffee, Cointreau or brandy.

This quantity will serve six people as a dinner party dessert, or four hungry chocolate lovers!

Chris Mann
PAN-FRIED SCOTTISH VENISON

Chris Mann presents The Food and Drink Hour every Monday on his BBC Radio Cambridgeshire show Mann in the Morning, featuring local chefs, restaurateurs, producers and other personalities from local food and drink businesses. Born in Scotland, Chris travelled the world as a foreign correspondent but for the last 15 years has lived in Cambridgeshire. His radio programme is on 9-12 every weekday.

Preparation time: 20 minutes | Cooking time: approx. 1 hours 30 minutes | Serves 4

Ingredients

800g venison loin

400g potatoes, thinly sliced

2 cloves of garlic, chopped

600ml double cream

100g wild mushrooms, sliced

50ml white wine vinegar

50ml water

50g sugar

16 cherry tomatoes on the vine

750ml good beef stock

400ml good red wine

1 stick of cinnamon

1 star anise

4 whole cloves

12 baby carrots, peeled and washed

100ml olive oil

Salt and pepper

Method

Cut the venison loin into four even pieces and season on all sides. Layer the sliced potatoes, chopped garlic, cream, salt and pepper into a roasting dish. Cook at 180°c for 45-50 minutes. Meanwhile, put the vinegar, water and sugar into a small pan, bring to the boil and reduce by half, then leave to cool a little and add the sliced mushrooms to pickle them. When the potatoes are cooked, turn the oven off, brush the tomatoes with a little oil and put into oven until serving. Put a little oil into a pan over a high heat and sear the venison – leaving it a little rare – then remove it from the pan and leave to rest. Put the stock and wine into a pan with the spices, bring to the boil and reduce to a smooth jus. Pour a little oil into a pan and sauté the baby carrots.

To plate

Divide all the vegetables and potato bake onto four dinner plates. Carve the venison and place in the centre. Spoon or pour over the jus to taste and enjoy.

Chris Mann

BBC
CAMBRIDGESHIRE
96.0 FM | 95.7 FM | DAB
bbc.co.uk/cambridgeshire

Chris Mann
APPLE AND CINNAMON CRUMBLE

Apple and cinnamon crumble with Cambridge vanilla cream

Preparation time: 15 minutes | Cooking time: 40 minutes | Serves 4

Ingredients

400g cooking apples, peeled and thickly sliced

75g dark brown sugar

¼ tsp ground cinnamon

50g unsalted butter, melted

150g soft brown breadcrumbs

200ml Cambridge double cream

1 vanilla pod

25g icing sugar

25ml apple brandy

Method

In a pan combine half of the melted butter, all the apple, half of the brown sugar and half of the cinnamon. Cook until the apples are soft and then divide between four dishes or ramekins. Mix the breadcrumbs with the rest of the brown sugar, butter, and cinnamon in a bowl. Sprinkle the crumble over the cooked apple and bake for 15-20 minutes until golden brown.

To serve

Mix the double cream with the seeds from the vanilla pod, icing sugar and apple brandy and serve on the side of the hot apple crumble.

Everything but the
KITCHEN SINK

A shop, deli, take-away kitchen and local collective – Country Kitchen comes under many names but is at heart a place to find and enjoy wonderful Cambridgeshire-made food and lovely things for the home.

Country Kitchen is an award-winning venture run by a collective, comprised of six women from neighbouring villages, who each contribute to this 'Aladdin's Cave' of a very special local shop. Liz, Heather, Jill, Claire, Kate and Alex all took a relatively new step into food and retail with the united aim of "providing a service to the community". This service mainly comes in the form of deliciously fresh food and drink to take away, from the jam-packed shelves of the deli-style section to the counter boasting homemade sausage rolls, soups, hot drinks and treats. There's a treasure trove of gifts for sale as well, including hampers which can be made up to order, featuring the work and craftsmanship of local artists.

Having celebrated their fifth year in 2018 and recently expanded the kitchen, the Country Kitchen team can also offer a whole range of homemade meals – even baked or prepared in customers' own dishes! – as well as fresh fish on Fridays from the local day boat catch, fruit and vegetables from nearby producers, artisan bread, cheese and charcuterie…you really have to visit the shop and explore all its wonders to discover all the edible treats in store. There are even gluten-free, dairy-free and sugar-free ranges, plus beer from local microbreweries and wine from specialist merchants to wash it all down with.

The sourcing and stocking ethos is broadly Cambridgeshire focused, celebrating the best of what's on the doorstep, but includes quality products from around the world too. The six committed partners will go the extra mile to search out sustainable and ethical options, so when a regular asked for quinoa that wasn't shipped from overseas, for example, they found a British-grown crop of the popular grain through Cambridge Organic Food Co. It's always an initial question of what's in season and what can be sourced as close as possible at the best quality, which both help to keep costs down – this is an important consideration at Country Kitchen as they're supporting and engaging with the rural and village communities.

Past the cheerful blue shopfront, the cooking smells are the most commented on aspect of the first few steps into Country Kitchen. It's hard to resist the aromas of freshly baked goodies and traybakes, whether you're putting together a family meal or a dinner party, and with everything you need to put wonderful food and drink on the table plus more besides, you won't have to!

Country Kitchen
THAI ROASTED RED PEPPER AND SWEET POTATO SOUP

My Dad always taught me that the basis of a good soup is the onions and sweating the vegetables before you add the stock. On my travels I visited a small farm shop in Suffolk while out with my daughter; this is my version of a yummy soup I had that day.

Preparation time: 20 minutes | Cooking time: 20-30 minutes | Serves 6

Ingredients

1 tbsp garlic oil

450g onions, peeled and chopped

500g carrots, peeled and chopped

480g jar roasted red peppers, drained

1 kg sweet potato, peeled and chopped

1 red chilli

5cm piece of ginger, peeled and chopped

1 vegetable stock cube, dissolved in a litre of water

400ml tin of coconut milk

Salt and pepper, to taste

Method

Heat the oil, add the onions and sweat until soft. Add all the other vegetables, the chilli and ginger, and then pour in the stock and coconut milk. Bring to the boil and then simmer until all the vegetables are soft. Blend with a hand blender until smooth. Add salt and black pepper to your taste.

To serve

Ladle the hot soup into bowls, top with croutons and a drizzle of oil.

For a lower-carb version of this recipe, use butternut squash instead of sweet potato.

Farm to FORK

Food is at the heart of Dog In A Doublet from the gastropub, deli and catering to the farm that provides much of their produce.

John and Della bought what is now a Cambridgeshire destination for food lovers as a derelict building, but after a six month refurbishment in 2011, Dog In A Doublet opened once more. Buying the traditional country pub as well as farmland with the potential to create much more allowed the couple to combine their passions for great food and well cared for animals, so they sold their home and moved everything – Della's horses included – to the site. "We put everything into it; this was a labour of love for us," says John, who saw a need for a pub with great food and wanted to show people what his individual style of cooking was all about.

The expression farm to fork was never truer than at Dog In A Doublet, where if customers ask about the provenance of the pork in their sausages and mash, John can point out the window at the rare-breed pigs. Meat and dairy from across the River Nene, which runs past the front of the pub, provide the basis for good old English 'pub grub' with a little twist. Fish and chips, for example, come with samphire in katsu curry sauce and a mango tartare, showcasing John's love of fusion food. He travelled all over the world as a civil engineer, which was his career path before reaching the quarter finals on Masterchef, and has always been keen to re-imagine simple dishes with great ingredients.

John's head chef James (formally of Gordon Ramsays' Maze and the award-winning Nags Head in Abercych) has now taken the reins in the kitchen, and is just as enthusiastic about pushing the restaurant and pub food to the next level, using modern techniques and high-end ideas to cook for a local Cambridgeshire audience, as well as the many visitors to whom Dog In A Doublet's renown has spread across the three counties it borders and even overseas.

The geographically striking location hosts much more than a gastropub for its visitors near and far. Diners can also visit the deli, stay in the B&B (with its balconies for the striking sunsets) or glampsite (with its giant tents based on the local Bronze Age settlements), and families will enjoy the opportunity to meet the farm animals. Dog In A Doublet also offers catering services including "the best hog roast you'll ever have" so whatever the occasion, John and Della welcome everyone to visit this Peterborough institution for food, drink and a dining experience with a difference.

Dog in a Doublet
BUTTERNUT SQUASH CURRY

This recipe is often on the menu as Dog In A Doublet's vegan 'pub' curry. Its South East Asian sauce can be accompanied by prawns in a Keralan style, but this is art not science so don't be afraid to swap and adapt ingredients to suit.

Preparation time: 15 minutes | Cooking time: 40 minutes | Serves 4

Ingredients

For the textures of jasmine rice:

110g jasmine rice

For the curry sauce:

1 tbsp toasted sesame oil

50g Thai shallots, finely chopped

1 inch of fresh ginger, finely grated

1 clove of garlic, crushed

6 kaffir lime leaves, gently bruised

2 lemongrass stalks, very finely sliced

1 can of coconut milk

40g palm sugar

1 tbsp coriander root, finely chopped

Salt and white pepper, to taste

For the butternut squash:

300g butternut squash, peeled, deseeded and 1cm cubed

1g xanthan gum

2g Jersey sea salt

5g flour

5g black sesame seed

5g onion seeds

For the accompaniments:

1 pak choi

1 red pepper

1 courgette

To finish:

5g granulated sugar

5g Jersey sea salt

1 small red chilli, deseeded

Fresh coriander, finely chopped

Optional extras (for non-vegans):

1 tbsp coconut oil

1 tsp brown mustard seeds

1 tsp ground fenugreek

A pinch of asafoetida

Small handful of fresh curry leaves

1 tbsp caster sugar

1 tsp fish sauce

4 (per person) of the biggest prawns you can get, peeled, and deveined

Method

For the rice puffs

Boil 10g of the jasmine rice in water until cooked. Drain and transfer onto greaseproof paper. Put in a dehydrator, or an oven, at 56°c until dried out (this will take about 6 hours). To make the rice shard, boil 50g of the jasmine rice in water until sticky, and then dry in exactly the same way as the rice puffs. Boil the remaining rice until cooked.

For the curry sauce

Put the oil in a medium-hot pan, then add the shallots, ginger, garlic, lime leaves, coriander root and lemongrass. Stir for 1-2 minutes then add the coconut milk and palm sugar. Turn down the heat and simmer until the sauce is reduced by half. Season to taste.

For the butternut squash purée and fried pieces

Place all the cubed butternut squash in a saucepan and cover with water. Add a pinch of sea salt and put on a high heat to boil until very soft. Place two thirds of the butternut in a blender and blitz until smooth, add the xanthan gum and then blitz again for about 1 minute until silky and smooth.

Drain the remaining butternut and roll the cubes in flour, then dip them into a flour and water mix (this should be the consistency of single cream) and finally roll them in the seeds.

Cut the base off the pak choi and discard, peel half a courgette into long ribbons until you get to the seeds, core and deseed the red pepper and then slice it thinly. Blend the sugar, salt and sliced chilli together.

To finish

In a deep fat fryer, fry the rice shard, rice puff and butternut squash pieces at 180°c until crispy. Fry the vegetables in a very hot pan to just colour them, and then reheat the rice, butternut purée and curry sauce. Arrange everything on the plate. Finish with the chilli sugar and fresh coriander.

Optional extras (for non-vegans)

In a very hot wok, add the oil then each of the spices. Allow to brown and sizzle and then add the prawns. Keep them moving to cook, then when just done add the sugar to caramelise. Add the fish sauce and then quickly remove from the pan and serve on top of the bowls of curry.

Dream DESSERTS

From buttery breakfast pastries to macaron flavours you've rarely seen, Dulcedo Patisserie is a place where the sweet-toothed will find themselves in seventh heaven.

Artfully created desserts and unusual treats, taking inspiration from the world over, are the main event at Dulcedo Patisserie. Through the careful consideration and development of tastes and textures, everything is made to meet a unique and exceptional standard by patissier Andrew and his partner Joanna, who own and set up the business. With 20 years of experience working in fine dining restaurants and world-renowned colleges across the UK and abroad, Andrew's passion for patisserie is evident in the sheer detail of Dulcedo's beautiful glass display cabinet of delights.

Their repertoire is always evolving, with seasons epitomised in vibrant floral flavours throughout spring and decadent rich chocolates for rainy winter days. From freshly made pastries to picture-perfect glazes, Andrew and Joanna wholeheartedly believe in constantly pushing the envelope and evoking curiosity in both new customers and regulars to sample their new innovations. Stretching the boundaries of what can be done in baking, Dulcedo has earnt its reputation in the Cambridge community at the forefront of modern patisserie, charting new and wonderful ways to encapsulate flavour, substance and finesse.

While Dulcedo's doors are always open for a browse and a treat to takeaway, the patisserie's services are also available for private hire for events, from weddings to business lunches. Upon request, Andrew and Joanna are more than happy to personalise their macaroons and chocolates, and have extensive knowledge to share on helping customers pair patisserie with drinks and menus. Dulcedo follow a simple but genuine ethos; the best quality experiences come from using the best quality ingredients, so Andrew and Joanna support local suppliers and producers too, using their produce in over 100 handmade creations.

Having worked as head pastry chef at Cambridge University's Clare College, Andrew aims to begin passing on his own skills now he has the freedom to direct and invent on his own terms. Training and developing aspiring patissiers is the next step for Andrew, alongside continuing the success of Dulcedo. He hopes to host evening events in the near future at the patisserie, which would feature a tasting menu and showcase a more formal side to his cookery. Doing something new and exciting is what "keeps you going", says Andrew, so there will never be a shortage of novelty at Cambridge's very own sweet sensation.

Dulcedo Patisserie
GIANDUJA

Gianduja is an indulgent hazelnut mousse filled with a caramelised ganache and caramel crunch; an incredible combination of rich flavours and contrasting textures.

Preparation time: 2 hours | Cooking time: 10 minutes | Serves 5-8

Ingredients

For the ganache:

10g caster sugar

31g cream

Pinch of salt

1 vanilla pod, seeds scraped

15g 70% dark chocolate

10g milk chocolate

30g butter

For the praline:

18g sugar

20g hazelnuts, roasted

4g cocoa butter, melted

For the gianduja mousse:

180g cream

80g eggs, beaten

32g sugar

1¼ leaves gelatine

80g gianduja

80g milk chocolate

For the crunchy base:

40g sugar

10ml water

100g milk chocolate

100g gianduja

10g oil

2g salt

For the glaze:

180g sugar

24ml water

20g glucose

120g cream

64g cocoa powder

3 leaves gelatine

For the garnish:

Gold leaf

Milk chocolate squares

Hazelnuts, roasted and halved

Method

For the ganache

Make a dry caramel by putting the sugar in a pan and heating over a gentle flame until it has melted and turned amber. De-glaze the pan with cream, and then add the vanilla and salt. Heat and cool to around 30°c. Melt the chocolate and the butter together, combine this with the caramel and then freeze in 20ml silicon moulds. Don't fill them right to the top; leave a thin gap.

For the praline

Make a dry caramel in the same way as before, add the roasted hazelnuts and blend everything together to make spreadable mixture. Put this on top of the ganache in each mould and refreeze.

For the mousse

Whip the cream until soft. Heat the eggs and sugar to 60°c, then whip on a high speed and melt in the gelatine. Fold this mixture into the cream, melt the gianduja and chocolate, and then combine that with the mousse by gently folding together. Pour the mousse into 100ml silicon moulds, filling them half way up. Place a frozen ganache, topped with the praline, inside each one and then fill the mould with the remaining mousse, leaving a very small gap at the top.

For the crunchy base

Make a caramel in the same way as above, adding the water to make sure it doesn't caramelise, and then when the caramel is amber coloured pour it over the chocolate and gianduja in the bowl of an electric mixer or food processor. Beat the caramel into the chocolate, adding the oil and salt as it combines, until you have a nice crunchy spreadable mixture.

For the glaze

Combine the water, sugar, cream and glucose. Heat to 102°c, add the cocoa powder and then boil again. Blend with a hand held blender, add the gelatine and blend again. Pass the glaze through a sieve, then when it has cooled to 40°c pour the glaze over the frozen gianduja.

To finish

Let the mousse thaw out and then serve the gianduja to your very impressed guests! This dessert goes very well with strawberries and cream for a little extra flourish.

Variety is the Spice
OF LIFE

Husband and wife team Gregg and Anna Thorne have created a café and deli that brings together everything they are passionate about: food that's full of exciting flavours, designed for sharing and enjoying with family and encouraging people to try something new.

Gregg and Anna Thorne set up Elder Street Café & Deli just outside the historic market town of Saffron Walden, bringing their diverse culinary experiences to the Cambridgeshire-Essex border. Gregg hails from the Isle of Wight, and Anna is originally from the Zachodniopomorskie region in northern Poland, but the couple share a love of travel and food inspired by flavours from all over the world. The café menu reflects this association of culture and cuisine, and is uniquely varied with the aim of encouraging customers to try and share new culinary experiences with family and friends.

Elder Street is the product of six years' hard work by Gregg and Anna and investment in their staff, suppliers and customers. Two of the chefs started as washer-uppers and have now completed apprenticeships with Cambridge Regional College, who awarded the café and deli Employer of the Year in 2017. Gregg and Anna also take great pride in representing their local suppliers, many of whom are from the local farming community and have since become friends. Great Garnett's Farm provides naturally reared, delicious pork, which features in many of the café dishes, and Honeyhouse honey – produced practically on the doorstep –

is another popular ingredient in their recipes. They also have the luxury of their own authentic Italian cheese guru who sources the best varieties in person!

The Elder Street ethos is to produce as much as possible on site and evolve the menu as seasonal availability and quality changes. Gregg and Anna are family-oriented – having a young son who is a budding cook himself – so love to design dishes that are fun, educational and perfect for sharing. Influences from Poland, Italy, Greece, and northern Africa (to name just a few) sit comfortably alongside the more traditional fare. Some of the most popular options include the impressive range of 'signature sarnies', as well as classic jacket potato lunches and cream teas.

Building on all these influences, Gregg and Anna host various events at the café throughout the year, turning the hustle and bustle of the daytime into an atmosphere that suits everything from live opera to Cuban carnivals. The combination of culture, food and music is at the heart of Elder Street Café and Deli, making each visit – day or evening, breakfast or lazy weekend afternoon – an experience to savour.

Elder Street Café and Deli

CATCHER IN THE RYE

This is our take on a classic American deli sandwich, with a few tweaks of our own. Gregg first discovered a 'Catcher in the Rye' in 2006 while dining at the famous Serendipity restaurant in the upper east side of New York City. The sandwich's name is broadly linked to the classic JD Salinger novel. 'Catcher' relates to the Russian dressing used in the sandwich and 'Rye' is the type of bread in which the filling is served. Traditionally the ingredients would include American semi-hard Muenster cheese – an imitation of the washed rind Munster cheese from Alsace, France – but as Muenster is not readily available in the UK, we use the original Alsatian Munster cheese. Whenever the 'Catcher in the Rye' features on the Elder Street menu it outsells any of our other signature sarnies!

Preparation time: 15 minutes | Serves 2

Ingredients

For the Russian dressing:

4 tbsp mayonnaise

1 tbsp tomato ketchup

½ tsp Worcestershire sauce

¼ tsp Tabasco sauce

1 tbsp fresh horseradish, grated

1 large gherkin, finely diced

1 tsp vodka

For the sandwich:

1 head of gem lettuce

6 vine cherry tomatoes, halved

4 thick cut slices of rye or malted bread

4 slices treacle cured black bacon

1 smoked chicken breast, sliced

1 Petit Munster cheese, sliced

Method

For the Russian dressing

Combine all of the ingredients thoroughly. Any extra dressing can be kept in an airtight container in the fridge for up to one month.

To construct the sandwich

Break the leaves of the gem lettuce into smaller pieces and put them in a mixing bowl. Add the halved cherry tomatoes and one tablespoon of Russian dressing. Toss gently; the key is to dress the salad without drowning it.

Place the black bacon under the grill until crispy. Toast the bread, and butter it while still warm. To build the sandwich, divide the dressed salad between the two sandwiches, top with a layer of the sliced smoked chicken, add the Munster cheese, and finally place the hot bacon on top to melt the cheese. Sandwich the filling with toasted, buttered bread and enjoy!

Elder Street Café and Deli

SPICY LAMB MEATBALLS

At Elder Street we like to keep our cuisine simple but perfectly authentic and full of flavour, creating our versions of the classics. A huge amount of research and planning goes into not only our menus but also our recipes. We introduced pork mince here in addition to the lamb to prevent the meatballs drying out during cooking, making them succulent and juicy. The Serrano ham and smoked paprika provide immense depth of flavour, making each mouthful sensational. This dish is great for sharing with family and is ideal for preparing in advance.

Preparation time: 1 hour | Cooking time: 20 minutes | Serves 4

Ingredients

For the tomato sauce:

2 tbsp olive oil

3 banana shallots, finely diced

2 cloves of garlic, grated

1 small red chilli, finely diced

400g chopped tomatoes

100ml dry sherry

100ml chicken stock

1 dried bay leaf

½ tsp sea salt

Pinch of ground black pepper

For the meatballs:

30g breadcrumbs

2 tbsp milk

350g lamb mince

150g pork mince

100g serrano ham, finely diced

1 egg yolk

¼ tsp ground nutmeg

½ tsp dried oregano

½ tsp cracked black pepper

½ tsp sea salt

½ bunch of flat leaf parsley, finely chopped

2 cloves of garlic, grated

1 tsp ground cumin

1 tsp ground coriander

½ tsp smoked paprika

2 tbsp olive oil

To serve:

½ bunch of flat leaf parsley, roughly chopped

Method

For the aromatic tomato sauce

Place a thick-bottomed saucepan over a medium heat and add the olive oil. Once the olive oil is warm enough, add the shallots, garlic and fresh chilli. Sweat until soft and translucent without colouring. Add all of the remaining ingredients to the pan, stirring to combine. Reduce the heat to low and simmer for 1 hour, stirring occasionally, until the sauce has thickened.

For the meatballs

Combine the breadcrumbs and milk and leave to stand for 5 minutes, so the breadcrumbs absorb the milk. Mix all the other ingredients together thoroughly and then stir in the soaked breadcrumbs. Using a 2cm metal cutter, press rounds out of the meatball mixture and shape to make approximately 24 meatballs. Place a non-stick frying pan on a high heat and add the olive oil. Once the oil is hot, add the meatballs to the pan in small batches. Sear and colour the meatballs on all sides, then transfer them to a suitable oven dish. Pour the hot tomato sauce over the meatballs and place in a preheated oven at 180°c for 8-10 minutes to finish cooking.

To serve

Garnish the dish with roughly chopped flat leaf parsley. We recommend serving the meatballs with homemade patatas bravas, and a salad of gem lettuce and diced feta cheese dressed with lemon and cumin spiked yoghurt.

Elder Street Café and Deli

MOROCCAN SHELLFISH AND CHICKPEA BROTH

In his late teens, Gregg spent his summer holidays working in a small restaurant in northern France but didn't realise at the time that what would influence and educate him more was living with a French-Algerian family and experiencing their culture and traditions first hand. Gregg is still very fond of communal cooking and dining, reflected in the family feast sharing section on Elder Street's menu. North African cuisine uses spices, but is more aromatic than hot – this recipe is a great example of this tendency. The broth can be prepared in advance making the final preparation convenient and a delicious meal ready in minutes.

Preparation time: 30 minutes | Cooking time: 5-10 minutes | Serves 4

Ingredients

For the broth:

2 tbsp olive oil

1 tsp coriander seeds

1 tsp fennel seeds

2 red chillies, deseeded and finely diced

1 tsp sugar

1 tsp ground turmeric

400g chopped tomatoes

150ml dry white wine

600ml fish stock

2 cloves of garlic, finely sliced

¼ tsp sea salt

¼ tsp cracked black pepper

400g cooked chickpeas

8 fresh king scallops, roe removed

12 fresh raw shell on tiger prawns

600g fresh mussels, cleaned

Chopped coriander or coriander cress, to garnish

Method

Place a thick-bottomed saucepan on a medium heat. Add the olive oil, coriander seeds, fennel seeds, red chillies and sugar. Cook while stirring until fragrant. Add the ground turmeric and cook for a further 2 minutes, stirring continuously. Add the chopped tomatoes, white wine, fish stock and sliced garlic. Stir to combine, bring to the boil, reduce the heat and simmer for 15 minutes. Season the broth. Add the chickpeas, followed by the scallops, tiger prawns and mussels. Cover the pan with a lid or plate and increase the heat to steam the shellfish. After a couple of minutes remove the lid and gently stir the broth. Once the prawns have turned pink, the mussels have opened and the scallops are just starting to become firm, the broth is ready.

To serve

Divide equally between four serving bowls. To garnish, sprinkle over some chopped coriander or coriander cress. Serve with homemade warm flatbreads seasoned with ras el hanout.

All Mapped OUT

Husband and wife team David and Caroline turned their love of travel into a deli, café and shop that will take you on a delicious journey of food and drink through Cambridgeshire and beyond...

The Geographer is a colourful and eclectic foray into great quality food and gifts, whether you pop in for coffee and cake, lunch or to pick up a special present and card. Creating a destination of this kind was the brainchild of Caroline and David, who spent a year travelling after they married and discovered a shared ambition to go places in the world of independent foodie businesses. While exploring abroad, they came across a café in Malaysia called The Geographer, which stuck with them not least because David is a geographer himself. On returning to their home country, fate seemed to step in when they found the ideal building to house their concept; it used to be a travel agent and was full of maps!

Naming their new venture The Geographer was a perfect homage to the whole journey towards its opening, complete with plenty of globe-themed décor and beautiful gifts, including locally made bags and candles, ceramics and homeware. The café menu is inspired by global cuisines too, and features ingredients imported from Europe alongside produce from the surrounding area, such as fresh bakes from Cobs Bakery, wholefoods from Arjuna – a long-standing Cambridge co-operative – and wine from Cambridge Wine

Merchants. Part of Caroline and David's ethos is to have anything used in the café, from breakfast to afternoon tea, available to buy from them. This includes a range of The Geographer's own wines, preserves and gifts plus the top-quality coffee from London's Nude Roastery that they are proud to stock and serve with a nibble; Portuguese custard tarts, Italian cannoli, or a slice of homemade cake all go down rather well!

Caroline and David love that The Geographer's customers can come for lunch, stay for a browse, and go home with a hearty meal to feed the family. They cater for events too – sometimes their own, when hosting an evening art or craft workshop or tasting – so make their food fresh in the café kitchen. Though The Geographer is in the midst of the pretty twinned villages of Histon and Impington, it's actually only a mile or so out from Cambridge's city centre. Lots of the locals are familiar faces for Caroline and David now, but the delights of the café, deli and shop are still waiting to be discovered by anyone who wants to see and eat their way around the world on their own doorstep!

The Geographer
SPANISH CHICKEN, CHORIZO AND BEAN STEW

We first served this stew at a Spanish-themed Supper Club at The Geographer and it went down so well that it now features amongst our range of frozen meals to cook at home. It's incredibly easy but tastes amazing; all the flavours from the chorizo infuse the rest of the ingredients, making a really hearty stew that tastes even better warmed up the next day!

Preparation time: 15 minutes | Cooking time: 45 minutes | Serves 4

Ingredients

400g (about 4) chicken thighs, with skin on

2 tbsp olive oil

Salt and pepper

1 onion, roughly chopped

200g chorizo sausage, diced

1 tsp smoked paprika

1 large potato, peeled and diced

2 carrots, peeled and diced

400g tin of chopped tomatoes

500ml hot vegetable or chicken stock

400g tin cannellini beans, drained and rinsed

100g baby spinach leaves

Handful of chopped parsley

Method

Preheat the oven to 200°c. Rub the chicken thighs with half of the oil, season with salt and pepper and then bake in the oven for around 35 minutes or until cooked throughout and the juices run clear. While the chicken is in the oven, peel and prepare the vegetables.

Heat the remainder of the oil in a large pan. Soften the onion on a gentle heat for 5-10 minutes.

Turn the heat up a little, add the chorizo sausage and paprika and cook for a further 5 minutes, stirring regularly. Tip in the diced potato and carrots and stir to coat them in oil. Add the tin of tomatoes and the stock, bring to the boil, and then reduce the heat to a gentle simmer. Cover and cook for 20 minutes, stirring occasionally, or until the vegetables are tender.

When the chicken is cooked and not too hot to handle, remove the skin from the thighs and then shred the chicken off the bone with your fingers. Add the shredded chicken and cannellini beans to the stew, turn up the heat and simmer for a further 5 minutes or until piping hot throughout.

To serve

When you're ready to eat, stir through the baby spinach leaves, spoon the stew into bowls and sprinkle over some chopped parsley. Serve with some crusty white bread and a glass of Rioja!

All Agog About
THE GOG

The Gog has grown from humble roots on a family farm into a Cambridgeshire destination, renowned for high-end specialist produce sold by people with real passion for sharing their love of great food and drink.

The story of The Gog's success starts and continues with one hard-working family. In 1919, the great grandfather of current managing director, Charles Bradford, came to the farm on the Gog Magog Hills and began a long-standing heritage rooted in the land that would be preserved and diversified by his son, grandson and great grandsons. Food retailing began when Colin Bradford started selling a surprise crop of mushrooms from the gate with an honesty box in the late 1960s, and after returning to help their parents with the business in 2004 his sons Charles and Marcus transformed the farm.

From the beginning, Charles focused on expanding the retail element while Marcus learnt butchery, and today they run a multi-award-winning farm shop that comprises a butchers, cheese shop, grocers, deli and café. Two have turned into over fifty trained and passionate people who are following careers there, and it's thanks to this emphasis on sourcing and the development of real food crafts that The Gog has steadily gained a reputation for brilliant produce including a range of sausages, some truly legendary Scotch eggs, Neal's Yard cheeses and much more. "People just love really great-tasting food, and there is a genuine appetite for fantastic ingredients," says Charles.

While the ambition and strong values of The Gog speak for themselves to the hordes of loyal customers, there's been plenty of national acclaim heaped on the shop and its staff. A Great Taste Golden Fork award for Best Farm Shop came hot on the heels of Farm Shop Small Retailer of the Year – as well as East Anglian Regional Winner accolades at the Farm Shop and Deli Awards in 2017 and 2018 – and since 2012, the tally of Great Taste awards for their products has reached 15!

It's always been important to the owners that the quality of the food and drink is matched by the expertise of their staff, and being able to tell customers exactly where the produce comes from goes hand in hand with curating fruitful relationships with suppliers. The Gog hosts regular events that showcase these small businesses, as well as The Gog Sundowners which are known for lots of music, beer and fun to celebrate the end of the working week during summer. Once people are a part of The Gog – be they regular customers, employees, family, Cambridgeshire producers – they really do contribute to and benefit from the community that holds the family business at its heart.

The Gog
FLAT IRON STEAK WITH CRISPY GARLIC POTATO BITES

A proper steak can be a thing of beauty, but it can be tricky to feed a crowd.
We love big sharing plates of food that everyone can tuck into and most of
this recipe can be prepared in advance, so you can spend more time with your
guests. Flat Iron is the American term for a great value cut that is often called
Feather Blade. It's a large piece of meat, so we prefer to cook it as a single piece
and share it out once it has been carved.

Preparation time: 20 minutes, plus 30 minutes chilling | Cooking time: approx. 2 hours | Serves 4

Ingredients

For the crispy garlic potato bites:

4 large baking potatoes

2 bulbs of garlic

Dried breadcrumbs

1 egg

Vegetable/sunflower oil for frying

For the salsa verde:

1 handful of flat leaf parsley

1 handful of basil

A few sprigs of rosemary, leaves removed (optional)

½ handful of capers

½ handful of gherkins

1 tbsp Dijon mustard

½ clove of garlic

8 tbsp wine vinegar

1 tbsp lemon juice

8 tbsp good olive oil

For the sharing steak:

1 flat iron steak (remove from the fridge a good hour before cooking)

4 fresh, bushy rosemary twigs

2 fat cloves of garlic

Large knob of butter

Method

For the crispy garlic potato bites

These can be prepared in advance and cooked while the steak is resting. Heat the oven to 160°c and prick the baking potatoes all over with a fork. Place them straight on the oven shelf to cook. After 30 minutes put the whole garlic bulbs on the rack as well and cook for a further 60 minutes. Allow the potatoes to cool a little, cut them in half and scoop out all the fluffy middles in to a large bowl. Squeeze as much of the gooey, roasted garlic into the potato as you can. Season with a good pinch of sea salt and lots of freshly ground black pepper. Mix well and place in the fridge for 30 minutes. When chilled, roll the potato mix into bite sized balls, dip in the beaten egg and then coat in the breadcrumbs. This amount makes approximately 20 bites.

To cook them, heat about 5cm of oil in a pan to 180°c (if you don't have a temperature probe then gently drop a small piece of bread into the pan, it should bubble vigorously if the oil is hot enough). Fry the balls in batches, remembering to check the oil temperature each time.

For the salsa verde

Put all the ingredients, apart from the oil, in a food processor and pulse until coarsely chopped, or roughly chop by hand. Add the oil two spoonfuls at a time and pulse until you get a chunky but pourable consistency.

For the sharing steak

Put a thick bottomed pan on a high heat. Rub the steak with oil and generously season with salt and pepper on both sides. Heat a good tablespoon of oil in the pan and then lay the steak in. Turn the steak every minute for 6 minutes (so it has 3 minutes per side in total) and about halfway through cooking rub the butter all over the steak and stir the herbs around the pan. When done to your liking, take the meat out and place on a warm plate for 5-6 minutes to rest.

To serve

Slice the steak on a chopping board, pour the resting juices over the pieces and serve with the salsa verde drizzled over the top and crispy potato bites on the side.

The Gog
SOUTHERN FRIED CHICKEN WITH FRESH CHOP SALAD

Most recipes will have you scouring the supermarkets for buttermilk and brining the chicken overnight, but this is a super easy recipe with none of the pain; just ensure that you use good quality British chicken from a butcher and enjoy this simple feast with friends and family.

Preparation time: 20 minutes, plus marinating time | Cooking time: 10-20 minutes | Serves 4

Ingredients

For the southern fried chicken:

300ml milk

300ml plain yoghurt

2 eggs

4 tsp good quality Spanish paprika

4 lemons, zested

2 tsp dried thyme

2 tsp sea salt

2 tsp garlic granules (optional)

8 medium chicken thighs, bone in and skin on

500g plain flour

2 litres sunflower or groundnut oil

For the chop salad:

1 avocado

1 cucumber

2 little gem lettuces

8 spring onions

Small handful of dill

Small handful of mint leaves

2 tbsp good olive oil

½ lemon, juiced

To serve:

Handful of good cherry tomatoes, halved

Method

For the southern fried chicken

Mix the milk, yoghurt and egg together to make the 'buttermilk' and set aside. Mix the paprika, lemon zest, thyme, sea salt and garlic together. Coat the chicken pieces generously with the rub and leave to marinate for a little while. If cooking in batches, preheat the oven to 160°c to keep the fried chicken warm until ready to serve. Put the flour on a large plate and grind over lots of black pepper. Heat about 8cm of oil in a pan to 180°c (if you don't have a temperature probe then gently drop a small piece of bread into the pan, it should bubble vigorously if the oil is hot enough). Dip the seasoned chicken into the 'buttermilk' and then into the peppered flour. Gently drop the chicken into the oil. Don't overcrowded the pan as the temperature will drop, so cook the chicken in batches if necessary, checking the temperature of the oil to ensure it remains at 180°c after each batch. Cook for about 12 minutes or until the internal temp of the chicken is 73°c. Remove and drain on kitchen paper then place in the oven to keep warm until serving.

For the chop salad

This clean and crunchy salad can be made a couple of hours ahead of time. Roughly chop all the veg up into pieces about the size of your little fingernail. Finely chop the dill and mint and put the herbs in a bowl with the vegetables. Pour in the oil and lemon juice and season with a little salt and pepper. Mix it through and serve alongside the chicken with some juicy cherry tomatoes.

Rhythm and BREWS

Coffee, music and conversation are the order of the day at Hot Numbers two coffee shops, supplied with delicious freshly ground and roasted speciality grade Arabica coffee by their very own roastery.

Simon Fraser, the creator and founder of Hot Numbers Coffee, is a man of many interests and ambitions. He started out as an engineer, enrolled on a positive thinking course which prompted travels to Australia, where he studied saxophone and indulged his twin passions for music and great flat whites. On returning home to Cambridge, Simon was looking for a way to combine the two when he discovered his first venue just off the bustling Mill Road. The name was his tribute to a venerable record store nearby, and of course a reference to Simon's vision for the space; a meeting point for good music, good coffee and locals who enjoyed both.

The friendly, laid back coffee shop specialises in fantastic brunches devised by head chef Adam Wilkinson – all the classics with some intriguing international flavours sneaking in – and well as the menu of espresso and filter coffees. On weekends it opens late and plays host to live music with a general leaning towards jazz and blues. The combo proved so popular with the "lovely vibrant community" – part of what Simon enjoys about the area – that a couple of years later the time seemed right to open another shop and then a roastery. The Trumpington Street location is ideal for light lunch breaks and freshly made sandwiches, soups and salads to take away.

Though both shops have their own individual character, Simon emphasises that it's important for the food to match the quality of their coffee at both. The roastery team, headed up by Jonny, select and prepare the Coffea Arabica with a huge amount of care and research. They use state-of-the-art equipment and software to continually refine the process, and also enjoy experimenting with single-origin blends and different styles of brewing. Hot Numbers Coffee trains its own baristas at the roastery alongside wholesale and home users wishing to better understand their equipment and hone their barista skills, with kit and bags of beans available to buy, plus fresh coffee to enjoy there of course!

Simon likes to support local suppliers with his business, and has a loyal following of Cambridge cafés and restaurants who buy the coffee wholesale. Having scooped several awards recently, including being listed amongst Britain's top 30 'best and buzziest coffee shops' by The Telegraph in 2017, business is booming: Simon's eclectic interests have led him to create something coffee lovers and music buffs won't be able to resist!

Hot Numbers Coffee

Hot Numbers Coffee
FOR THE DAY: BREAKFAST BREW

Whether you are a brewing professional or a novice, the V60 brewer is
an extremely versatile bit of equipment. We love it for its simplicity and
affordability. This recipe is our personal favourite and is fail safe for brewing
to SCA gold cup standard. That said, feel free to experiment with different sizes
and recipes and have some caffeinated fun!

Ingredients

Equipment:

V60 size 02

Filter papers

Scales

Stirrer

Timer

Kettle

Ingredients:

Good quality filtered water

Your favourite coffee mug

Delicious fresh ground coffee

Method

Place the filter paper into the V60, wet the paper with warm water and then add 22g of
ground coffee into the V60. Place the V60 onto the device you would like to brew into
and zero/tare the scales. Once the water is boiled, start your timer and add 60g to the
coffee bed. Make sure to wet the coffee evenly. Mix the coffee gently to ensure this. After
30 seconds pour on the remaining 300g of water. Stir in a circular motion around four
times so the coffee and water mix is spinning. When the water level has dropped by half,
pick up the V60 and swirl then place it back on to your mug. Once all the water has left
the V60 you should be left with a flat bed of coffee.

If the water leaves the V60 very quickly you will need to make your grind finer until it
takes 2½-3½ minutes for your full brew time.

Pour and enjoy!

Hot Numbers Coffee
FOR THE NIGHT: COFFEE COCKTAIL

The perfect recipe to bring you down after a day of making coffee. We love the simplicity
and pure deliciousness of the recipe. Switch between either cold brew or espresso and
see which you prefer. We love using natural processed Ethiopian coffee beans for this
recipe as it adds an incredibly complex flavour to an already great cocktail.

Ingredients

30ml Ethiopian natural cold brew
or espresso

30ml brandy

30ml single cream

10ml simple syrup

To garnish:

Cocoa powder

Nutmeg, freshly grated

Ground cinnamon

Method

Add all the main ingredients to a cocktail shaker along with a handful of ice. Shake
vigorously and strain into a glass. Top with cocoa powder, nutmeg and cinnamon to taste.

The SCOOP

With an unrivalled list of flavours – from the familiar to the unique – and handmade creations made with exceptional ingredients, Jack is Cambridge's own ice cream and sorbet aficionado.

After many happy years working in the restaurant industry, which took him all over the world, Jack van Praag returned to his home town of Cambridge with a desire to create something different, so in 2011 he put everything he had into opening Jack's Gelato and hasn't looked back since. With a team of ten people over summer, and just three (including himself) who work all year round, Jack has turned an idea inspired by time spent in Italy visiting his father into a great success, dedicating his days to the cold stuff.

Pint Shop, The Gog and Hot Numbers are just a few of the Cambridge establishments featuring Jack's Gelato products, whose big, bold and clean flavours are an absolute delight. Jack is also the proud owner of three Pashley tricycles; these can be seen at public and private events, or simply out and about in the city. He has recently seen his business expand even further by supplying some top London locations, including Dover Street Market and the new Bridge Theatre, and there has been talk of opening a Jack's Gelato shop there in the future too.

At Cambridge's Bene't Street shop gelato fans can choose from between 12 to 16 flavours, which change daily from a total repertoire of well over 250 varieties and counting, all churned in the kitchen in front of everybody. It's no wonder that Jack has made a name for himself as a "culinary wizard" according to happy customers, who love the mixture of British classics – think vanilla; strawberries and cream; seasonal elderflower, damson or rhubarb – and the unexpectedly delicious , such as Earl Grey and plum sorbet or burnt milk chocolate.

All of Jack's ingredients come from a background of ethical and sustainable sourcing, whether it's milk from Jersey and Guernsey cows, Pump St chocolate, or even produce from Jack's own allotment. Jack still travels too, returning to Italy regularly and taking the opportunity to visit other countries once a year when the shop closes in January and February, finding inspiration and even bringing back ingredients to develop new recipes with. This development process is "great fun – it's one of the many things that keeps me excited" says Jack, and it's hard to think of a better way to spend your days than bringing fun and flavour to people in the form of such a delicious treat, made truly individual and special.

Jack's Gelato
COLD INFUSED COFFEE GRANITA

This is one of my absolute favourite quick desserts and is unbelievably simple. You can have a huge amount of fun (and create hugely different results) by experimenting with different coffee beans and different lengths of infusion, really making this recipe your own. My current favourite is the wonderful Costa Rican Coffee from the hugely talented Rory and Marcella at the Coffee Officina in Essex.

Preparation time: 10 minutes, plus 24-48 hours| Serves: 4-6

Ingredients

400ml water, preferably mineral or filtered

110g coffee beans

95g sugar

Whipped cream (optional)

Method

Start off by grinding your coffee. You can do this by using a hand or electric grinder; you could even resort to using a pestle and mortar or the end of a rolling pin and a chopping board or saucepan. Just bear in mind the coarser the grind; the longer the infusion time. I like a medium coarse grind.

Place your ground beans in a container with the water and then cover and refrigerate. The grinds will float, you can nudge things along by agitating them periodically. When you decide it is time to move to the next step (I would advise 24-48 hours) strain out the liquid gold by pouring through a coffee strainer, or a sieve lined with a chemical-free paper towel. Add the sugar and stir to dissolve, please note that if you use granulated this will naturally take longer than a finer-grained sugar. You are now ready to freeze the mixture. Transfer to a shallow dish, so that the liquid it is 1 to 3 cm deep, and place in the freezer. It will speed things up if you are able to pre-freeze the dish but it is by no means required.

When it starts to become firm you want to scrape the mixture with a fork and break it up. It may take an hour or it may take 3 or 4 hours to get to this stage; it depends on how cold and how large your freezer is. Continue with this process periodically until you have a beautiful crystalline texture throughout. I find it normally takes 2 to 3 rounds. It is now ready to serve but can be kept like this for a few hours (or even days, if needs be; but something will be lost the longer you store it) and broken up lightly before serving.

Serving suggestion

I love to serve this with a little lightly whipped cream – a pinch of sugar and possibly some freshly scraped vanilla seeds folded in with the cream will work wonders. Place a few spoonfuls of granita in your serving vessels, top with a cloud of whipped cream and serve.

Steak please, and make IT SNAPPY!

Johnsons of Old Hurst is all about the best from field to fork: provenance, animal welfare, flavour and the people who contribute to the process every step of the way.

Andy Johnson's family have been farming in the Cambridgeshire village of Old Hurst since 1899. He and his wife diversified their livelihood together, continually branching out over the years to bring customers a range of home-grown produce and fresh meat as well as a steakhouse, farm shop, and tea room. Everything is situated on the working farm and together comprises a thriving business. Andy's philosophy takes a "no holds barred approach" when it comes to the connection between the animals they rear and the meat they sell. He and the team feel they have a responsibility to educate people, aiming to help everyone understand and appreciate where their food comes from.

Traditional methods of farming are in evidence along with skilled butchery, bakery and cookery at Johnsons of Old Hurst. Pigs, cattle, sheep and deer keep rather exotic company with water buffalo, ostrich and Nile crocodiles, also part of Andy's herd! He runs a breeding programme with the crocodiles and primarily uses them as part of a highly efficient waste disposal system, allowing the farm shop and butchery to be more sustainable and environmentally friendly as well as conserving the endangered species. Crocodile feeding demonstrations form part of an exciting events programme at the farm and acres of surrounding nature reserve, making Johnsons a great place to spend a more unusual day out with the family, as well as shop and enjoy a bite to eat!

With 11 butchers on site, Johnsons can boast one of the largest fresh meat counters in the country, with 80% of produce reared on its own land. The farm shop offers its own corned beef, hams, bacon, and an incredible 28 flavours of sausage amongst a plethora of high quality products from carefully chosen suppliers, including over 50 British cheeses and beers, ciders, wines and spirits from up and down the country. Using every part of the animal is a natural approach for Andy; the pork pies, for example, use ground meat, lard for the hot water crust pastry and trotters for the jelly all from his own Welsh cross pigs.

This traceability means that staff are quick to pass on their in-depth knowledge to customers looking for advice or recipes, and people come from near and far – even journeying especially from London once a fortnight – to enjoy the experience at Johnsons. With yet more exciting projects underway, Andy has plenty more ambition and drive to continue investing in his guiding principles, taking his unique business in innovative directions that benefit all involved.

Johnsons of Old Hurst

PAN-ROASTED HAUNCH OF VENISON

Inspired by the farm's very own majestic deer – which are reared alongside various other animals on the grounds – and by Andy son's love of chocolate.

Preparation time: 20 minutes | Cooking time: approx. 1 hour | Serves: 2

Ingredients

For the roasted vegetables:

2 large carrots, peeled and sliced into batons

1 large parsnip, peeled and sliced into batons

1 dessert spoon of honey

2g thyme, chopped

For the Parmentier potatoes:

100ml olive oil

5g rosemary, chopped

Salt and pepper

2 large potatoes, peeled and diced into 2cm squares

For the red cabbage purée:

200g red cabbage, sliced

150ml red wine vinegar

300ml vegetable stock

2g fennel seeds

For the venison:

20ml olive oil

5g rosemary, chopped

Salt and pepper

2 x 200g venison haunch steaks

For the sauce:

200ml red wine

25g butter

10g blueberry jam

10g blueberries

10g 70% chocolate

To garnish:

Pea shoots

10g blueberries

Method

For the roasted vegetables

Preheat the oven to 180°c. While you are waiting for the oven to heat up, par boil the carrots and parsnips. When just starting to soften, take out the carrots and parsnips and place them in a baking tray. Add the honey and thyme and roast in the oven for 10-12 minutes.

For the Parmentier potatoes

Heat up the oil with the chopped rosemary and seasoning in a frying pan and gently fry the diced potatoes until they are golden brown. Then, place the potatoes in a separate baking tray and finish in the oven for 8-10 minutes.

For the red cabbage purée

Fill a saucepan with water and bring to the boil. Add the sliced cabbage, red wine vinegar, vegetable stock and fennel seeds and boil until soft. Drain the cabbage, blend it into a purée, adding some of the cooking liquor back in if necessary until the texture is smooth, and then set aside.

For the venison

Mix half of the olive oil with a little chopped rosemary, salt and pepper to taste. Rub this into the venison. Heat the rest of the olive oil in a frying pan on a medium heat and then add the seasoned venison. Cook for 3-4 minutes on each side (timing may vary depending on the thickness of the steaks) and place the venison to one side to rest. Slice into portions just before serving.

For the sauce

Pour the red wine into a clean frying pan and heat until it has reduced by about half. Add the butter, jam, blueberries and chocolate and stir until you have a thickened, glossy sauce.

To serve

Arrange the root vegetables and Parmentier potatoes in the centre of a plate and place the sliced venison on top. Spoon droplets of the red cabbage purée around the edge of the plate and pour over the red wine, blueberry and chocolate sauce. Finish off with the remaining blueberries and pea-shoots.

Bring on the BRUNCH

Husband and wife team Dominic and Elizabeth brought fun and flavour to the community with the opening of their quirky café on the edge of St Ives.

Dominic and Elizabeth already run an award-winning events business in Cambridgeshire, but had always wanted to open their own café too. When a space became available in the very building they work from, it seemed too fortuitous an opportunity to pass up, so in May 2016 the Little Acre Kitchen opened its doors. As big fans of the fast-expanding brunch scene, Dom and Elizabeth were keen to introduce the same variety and quality to daytime fare in their own town. The café quickly established itself as a community-friendly venue, hosting yoga classes and breakfasts on Saturdays, flower arranging workshops and regular supper clubs with specially designed cocktails to match.

The food ranges from health-conscious to indulgent, with popular examples being the Buddha bowls, sweetcorn fritters, and sourdough toasties. Little Acre Kitchen merges its relaxed café atmosphere with restaurant standards over the busy lunchtimes, making all food fresh to order. Handily, this also means that dishes are easily adaptable for those with various dietary requirements, though there are always a good few vegan options on the menu and the cake counter too. Dom and Elizabeth work closely with their chef Anna and manager Frankie to design the menu around produce that's in season locally, even swapping out dishes on a weekly basis.

Making the most of the surrounding countryside, the team work with nearby suppliers and producers who can help them use the best available meat, fruit, veg and drinks from the area. Johnsons of Old Hurst are their butchers, Kale & Damson deliver fresh fruit and vegetables, artisan tea from the Kandula Tea Company is a popular menu feature and they also stock Breckland Orchard 'Posh Pop'. It's partly down to the commitment Dom and Elizabeth have made to shop and support local that has earned them such a loyal customer base. They both really enjoy building relationships with people they see every week, who love having a place to go outside the city that feels up to the minute, as well as somewhere you know you'll be well fed!

Admiring comments are often directed at the café décor too, particularly the coffee machine which is so eye-catching it serves as a centrepiece! The modern, uncluttered and relaxed feel of Little Acre Kitchen reflects the 'simple but done well' approach that Dominic and Elizabeth have brought to both their businesses, garnering them awards and great reputations, but most importantly for them, real satisfaction and enjoyment in doing what they set out to achieve.

Little Acre Kitchen
SWEETCORN FRITTERS

The sweetcorn fritters have been a menu staple since opening, and continue to be one of our most popular dishes both during the week and for weekend brunch. Our sweetcorn fritters are an adaptation of a dish we had during a research trip to New York. We absolutely love the flavour and texture combinations of this dish, along with it's versatility; for instance if you don't like sweetcorn, substitute the fritters for sweet potato and red onion cakes, or butternut squash and sage to make it more of a dinner dish.

Chef's tip: I find that using frozen sweetcorn works best in this recipe, however tinned or fresh will work too. Make sure the corn is thoroughly defrosted and give it a good squeeze in a clean kitchen cloth to remove any excess water before using.

Preparation time: 15 minutes | Cooking time: 40 minutes | Serves 4

Ingredients

For the tomato salsa:

1 punnet of red and yellow cherry tomatoes

1 red onion

2 sprigs of coriander, finely chopped

½ red chilli, diced

Salt and pepper

4 tbsp olive oil

For the fritters:

500g frozen sweetcorn

1 bunch of spring onions

½ bunch of chives

175g plain flour

1 tsp baking powder

125ml whole milk

2 whole eggs

2 egg yolks

Salt and pepper

To serve:

Charred halloumi

Charred chorizo

1 avocado, smashed

1 poached egg per person

Sriracha

Method

For the tomato salsa

To make the tomato salsa quarter the cherry tomatoes and dice the red onion. Place them in a bowl and add the chopped coriander, diced chilli, salt and pepper to taste, and finish with a good glug of olive oil.

For the fritters

Defrost your sweetcorn and squeeze out any excess moisture using a clean kitchen cloth.

Finely slice the spring onions and chives, and combine the remaining fritter ingredients in a large mixing bowl, and mix well.

Heat a teaspoon of olive oil in a frying pan and place a tablespoon of the fritter mix into the pan (we portion three tablespoon-sized fritters per portion). Cook for 2 minutes on each side and then place in the oven for 5 minutes.

While the fritters are cooking chargrill the halloumi and chorizo.

Once cooked place three fritters on your plate, add your chorizo and halloumi, finish with bashed avocado, a poached egg and some sriracha.

Poynton in the right DIRECTION

Mark Poynton's recent experiences of cooking at prestigious events all over the world, as well as his background at Midsummer House and his own Michelin-starred restaurant in Cambridge, have influenced the next exciting chapter in the chef's eclectic career.

Mark Poynton entered the world of hospitality at the tender age of 15 when a friend's mother got him a job as a part-time waiter at the Queen Hotel in Chester. During his time there he became fascinated by the workings of the kitchen, and after just six months as a waiter he persuaded the hotel's executive chef, Ian McDowall, that he was serious about cooking and his career behind the stoves began. 18 months with Paul Kitching at the Michelin-starred Juniper restaurant in Altrincham followed, before Mark made a career-defining move by joining Daniel Clifford at Cambridge's two Michelin-starred Midsummer House. During his seven year tenure Mark worked his way up through the ranks; during which time the restaurant gained two Michelin stars and four AA rosettes.

His next step was the head chef position at Alimentum, which gained three AA rosettes within a year of Mark's arrival. Mark took over Alimentum in 2010, becoming chef-patron, and in 2012 the restaurant was awarded its first Michelin star. He's now planning to move forward from this success and launch himself into another new culinary venture for 2018. He's travelled extensively in the last couple of years, visiting a number of cities across India cooking for the British Council, then creating and producing a taster menu for 100 people at the International Bank in Singapore. Mark enjoys the influences that emerge from challenging yourself to experience new cuisines and says "it's good to see what everybody else is good at" rather than being too centred on the food you're used to.

Mark aims to base his dishes around one vegetable element, or a particular flavour, that reflects the most flavoursome produce for that time of the year. To him, seasonality encompasses far more than just your own locality and sourcing produce from wherever it grows best is just good sense. Opening up a new restaurant in Cambridge with a focus on the simple, most pleasurable aspects of dining – nothing more and nothing less than "delicious plates of food" as Mark puts it – will allow the ambitious chef to continue developing his individual style of cooking. A newsletter, which can be signed up to via his website, will provide the latest updates on his progress, so watch this space!

Mark Poynton
SALMON, NORI, HORSERADISH

The inspiration for this dish came from a meal I had at Geranium in Copenhagen, where I ate a cured pollock dish with burnt parsley. I chose seaweed as a core flavour for my own take on the idea, and the rest fell into place.

Preparation time: 30 minutes, plus 30 minutes freezing | Serves: 20

Ingredients

For the salmon:

1 whole salmon

Salt and nori powder

Dill oil:

1 bunch (approx. 100g) of dill

Pomace oil

For the buttermilk dressing:

200ml buttermilk

¼ bunch dill, chopped

1 tbsp black caviar

Dill oil

Lemon juice and salt, to taste

Horseradish ice cream:

600ml milk

100g milk powder

1 clove of garlic

120g egg yolk

70g sugar

30g fresh horseradish (finely grated)

Salt to taste

Method

For the salmon

Fillet, skin and pin-bone the salmon. Wash gently and then dry in a cloth. Make a brine for the salmon by mixing 10g salt into 100ml of cold water. You might have to double the amount depending on the size of the salmon. Cut each fillet into three strips and place in the brine for 20 minutes, then pat dry with a cloth. Heavily dust the salmon with nori powder and roll all six strips together in a flower pattern, ensuring an even thickness throughout. Tightly wrap in cling-film and freeze.

For the dill oil

Blanch (drop into boiling water) and refresh (plunge into iced water) the dill, and then dry thoroughly. Blend the dill with pomace oil; the dill should be five times the weight of the oil. Pass the flavoured oil through muslin and set aside until serving.

For the buttermilk dressing

Combine all the ingredients in a bowl or jug.

For the horseradish ice cream

Put all of the ingredients apart from the horseradish in a pan and heat gently until the mixture reaches 82°c. Blend the mixture in a blender, add the horseradish and blend again to incorporate. Churn the mixture in an ice cream machine, or freeze in a sealed container and stir every 20 minutes (this prevents ice crystals forming) until frozen.

To finish

Place some of the buttermilk dressing onto a plate. Slice the salmon from frozen and remove the cling film, and then season it with the dill oil and a little black pepper. Place the salmon onto the dressing and leave it to thaw (this should take approximately 15 minutes) then place a scoop of ice cream on top of the salmon to finish and serve immediately.

Mark Poynton
DUCK, CARROT, SZECHUAN

The inspiration for this dish is very Asian, but it has a French twist.
Think duck a l'orange with spicing.

Preparation time: 1 hour 30 minutes | Cooking time: 35 minutes | Serves: 12

Ingredients

For the duck breast:

6 duck crowns

Szechuan pepper

Maple syrup

Candied grapefruit peel:

Pink grapefruit peel, all pith removed

Icing sugar, to dust

For the duck sauce:

Duck bones, roasted

1½ litres dark stock

300ml Madeira, reduced to sauce consistency

1 shallot, finely sliced

¼ bulb of garlic

100ml pink grapefruit juice, reduced to sauce consistency

1 grapefruit, segmented and chopped into 5 pieces per segment

For the carrot purée:

1kg carrots, peeled and finely sliced

250g butter

For the baby carrots:

36 baby carrots

250g butter

200ml orange juice

For the granola:

40g maple syrup

100g feuilletine

50g oats

50g flaked almonds

4g salt

Method

For the duck breast

Pour one large ladle of boiling water over each duck crown five times to render the fat. Blow-torch the skin on a low flame until dark all over and then chill the duck. Make a brine by mixing 10g salt with 100ml water. Remove the breasts from the crown and place them in the brine for 30 minutes. Keep the trimmings for the sauce. Rinse and dry the breasts in cloth, then wrap each one in cling film to produce a uniform shape and vacuum pack. Toast the Szechuan pepper and add the maple syrup. Reduce and set aside for glazing the duck breasts just before serving.

For the candied grapefruit peel

Cover the peel with cold water and bring to the boil three times. Drain well and then dust with icing sugar. Toast in a dry pan to crystallise the sugar, then dehydrate in a low oven until candied.

For the duck sauce

Reduce the stock with the roasted bones to a sauce consistency and then pass through a fine sieve. Caramelise the garlic, add the shallots and lightly caramelise. Add stock, bring to the boil and skim, add wine. Bring back to the boil, skim, check consistency and pass through a fine sieve. Finish the sauce with the grapefruit segments, peel and juice just before serving.

For the carrot purée

Gently simmer the carrots in the butter and 250ml of water until completely cooked through. Blend it all together and then pass through a sieve to get a smooth purée.

For the baby carrots

Trim the tops off the carrots, leaving 2cm of the green part attached, and keep them to garnish the dish. Trim and peel each carrot to create a uniform shape. Cook in the butter and orange juice for 4 minutes from the point it comes to the boil, and then allow the carrots to cool in the emulsion. Reduce the emulsion to a glaze before serving.

For the granola

Slightly reduce the maple syrup in large pan. Add the dry ingredients and stir until they are lightly coated. Tip out the granola onto a baking tray and place in the oven at 180°c until toasted, turning every two minutes so it doesn't catch and burn.

To finish

Cook the duck breast in a water bath at 62°c for 30 minutes and then caramelise the skin with the maple syrup and Szechuan pepper glaze. Add the carrot purée to the plate and sprinkle with granola, slice each duck breast in half along the length and place these onto the granola. Place the warm baby carrots on top, pour some sauce over the duck and then finish the dish with the carrot tops.

Mark Poynton
BLACK FOREST

This dish, and many of my desserts, comes from family favourites – tried and tested recipes that have been reworked – and this is my variation on Black Forest gateaux. Buy the best chocolate you can for the best results.

Preparation time: 3 hours | Cooking time: 2 hours | Serves: 12

Ingredients

For the pliable ganache:

300g each of dark and milk chocolate

125ml double cream

50g glucose

200g butter

70g egg yolk

3g cocoa powder

4g salt

250ml double cream, semi-whipped

For the dehydrated sponge:

4 eggs

225g sugar

175g self-raising flour

50g cocoa powder

25g butter

For the kirsch syrup:

Liquid from the tinned cherries

100ml kirsch

For the beer cherries:

250g tinned cherries

1 bottle of cherry beer

For the chocolate tuile:

200g white fondant

200g glucose

90g dark chocolate

For the cherry tuile:

1kg black cherry purée

200g sugar

For the meringue:

200g sugar

70ml water

100g egg white

Method

For the pliable ganache

Melt the chocolate and, in a separate pan, boil the cream and glucose. Gently heat the butter on a low heat stirring till the butter tuns nut brown in colour and smells like hazelnuts. Cool as quick as possible to stop the butter from burning

Whisk the yolks with the cocoa and salt, and then slowly add the beurre noisette. Add the boiled cream mixture and then pour in the melted chocolate. Whisk until the ganache is cool enough for you to fold through whipped cream, and then spread it out on trays lined with cling film to set in the fridge. Before serving, portion the ganache into 5cm by 10cm rectangles.

For the dehydrated sponge

Beat all the ingredients together until light and fluffy, transfer into a greased and lined cake tin, and then bake in the oven at 180°c for 20 minutes. Allow to cool slightly in the tin and then turn out onto a wire rack. Portion the cake by tearing it and then dehydrate in an oven at low temperature until crisp. Rehydrate the cake pieces by pouring the kirsch syrup over the sponge 2 minutes before serving.

For the kirsch syrup

Mix the two ingredients and set aside.

For the beer cherries

Halve the cherries and put them into an extremely hot dry pan. Add the beer, then pour everything into a sieve. Discard the liquid and dehydrate the cherries in a low oven until crisp for 45 minutes.

For the chocolate tuile

Heat the glucose and fondant together until the mixture reaches 150°c. Add the chocolate and pour the mixture onto a non-stick tray (or greaseproof paper) to set. Break up and blend into a powder in a blender or food processor. Sieve the powder onto a clean tray using a template of any shape and bake at 180°c for 6 minutes. Let it cool and then break into shards.

For the cherry tuile

Blend the two ingredients in a blender until smooth, spread the mixture onto a non-stick surface and then dehydrate in a low oven until crisp and able to be lifted off the tray or greaseproof paper.

For the meringue

Boil the sugar with 70ml of water until the mixture reaches 118°c. Meanwhile, whisk the egg whites until they form stiff peaks. Pour the sugar syrup onto the whites and keep whisking until cool.

To finish

To serve, place a portion of ganache in the centre of the plate and carefully place a little of all the ingredients on top of and around the ganache, so every mouthful will include different flavours and textures. At the restaurant we serve this with a cherry beer sorbet and dark chocolate aero.

Maid with LOVE

The Mermaid at Ellington combines the cosy welcome of a traditional public house, with centuries of history in its beams and walls, and the freshest fusion flavours in modern cuisine.

As a chef, Nick Marriot had always wanted his own place, so when the opportunity arose to create a unique dining destination and bring an historic public house back to life, he jumped at the chance. The Mermaid was closed and not far from derelict when Nick first laid eyes on the building, but even so, he was determined to heal the "hole in the heart of the village". Three months later, having enlisted the help of Ellington's supportive residents, the bar opened just in time for Christmas Eve 2014 to much celebration. Once he'd revealed the beautiful original features during the refurbishments – including ship's timbers from which the pub got its name and old coins in the walls, stored there by the local American Air Force pilots who used them to buy their pints on return from missions – and made the kitchen operational, Nick began his new adventure with heaps of ambition.

Having started out as a professional rugby player, Nick's passion for cooking – in particular the Asian and African influences he brings to The Mermaid's menu – fast-tracked him into the world of Michelin-starred chefs at Paris House. He is now bringing more young chefs into the industry from unconventional backgrounds like his own, and shaping their knowledge and experience to create top-quality food that's affordable and accessible to everyone. Bringing this level of technical cooking to a quiet country pub often leads to customers walking away "happily shocked" after their meal, which gives Nick a lot of joy as he's been able to come back to what he knows and loves but make it something special with a twist on the usual.

The Mermaid offers à la carte dining, lunch meal deals, themed nights including Sirloin Tuesdays, Fish Wednesdays, Curry Thursdays and Friday Tastings, Sunday classics, children's options, special occasions and an entire alternative menu for those with vegan, gluten-free, dairy-free, vegetarian or any dietary requirements. The way Nick sees it, if you're going to run a place with a family feel and genuine love for what you do, it has to welcome everyone with open arms. This wholehearted approach extends right down to food prep, where the entire animal is used and all dishes are made from scratch to ensure they have control over each element that makes the final result look and taste amazing.

Experimenting, listening to his team, and diving in to the challenge head first, Nick has brought The Mermaid a new lease of life with food from around the world that defies and delights expectations.

The Mermaid at Ellington

ASIAN SOFT SHELL CRAB & KAFFIR LIME

At The Mermaid, we experiment with many foods around the world, Asian style techniques and flavours are one of our favourites. The dish is the only one to have stayed on our menu since we opened; due to its popularity we daren't take it off! The lemon and kaffir lime leaf purée adds a great zing and beautiful freshness.

Preparation time: 35 minutes | Cooking time: 10 minutes | Serves: 4

Ingredients

For the soft shell crab:

4 jumbo soft shell crabs

For the lemon and lime leaf purée:

6 whole lemons

100ml water

Pinch of saffron

10 kaffir lime leaves

160g sugar

100ml olive oil

For the tempura batter:

190g gluten-free self-raising flour

9g baking powder

125g cornflour

1 lemon, zested

6g salt

2g white pepper

345ml soda water

For the soy sauce:

100g stem ginger

100ml sesame oil

150ml soy sauce

Pinch of xanthan gum

Method

For the lemon and lime leaf purée

Using a knife, cut the lemon peel from the lemon. To blanch the lemon peel, place in a pan with cold water and bring to a boil. Strain and fill up again with cold water and bring to the boil. Do this seven times or until the peel has softened. Bring the 100ml of water to the boil with the saffron in, and then pour this into a food processor with the lemon peel, lime leaves and sugar. Blitz for 10 minutes until the purée is smooth, and then slowly pour in the oil with the processor on until incorporated.

For the tempura batter

Thoroughly mix all dry ingredients together then add the soda water to form a smooth batter.

For the soy sauce

Blitz all the ingredients in a food processor for 8 minutes.

To finish

Heat enough oil to 180°c in a large saucepan to deep fry the crabs. Dip each crab into the tempura batter and then gently drop them into the oil. Cook for 6 minutes per crab, turning once. Remove and place on kitchen towel to drain off the oil.

We like to serve the crab with a dehydrated chilli, crispy ginger and spring onion salad dressed with the soy sauce, along with some coriander prawn crackers. Any fresh salad goes well with the dressing though so include whatever your taste buds fancy!

Not Just a Midsummer
NIGHT'S DREAM

Visited by gastronomes far and wide, Midsummer House is Cambridge's most highly recognised fine dining experience, with two Michelin stars and a reputation for the drama and excellence of its food.

Under the watchful eye of chef patron Daniel Clifford, Midsummer House is a beautiful riverside restaurant overlooking Midsummer Common, which has held two Michelin stars since 2005 and has recently undergone a kitchen expansion and restaurant refurb. Bringing the restaurant up to the standard it maintains today – often in challenging conditions to say the least – has been a labour of love for Daniel. The Victorian villa stands on the banks of the River Cam and has flooded twice since its first restoration. The devastation caused over the two consecutive winters is undetectable now, since the building has been upgraded to comprise a world-class kitchen, an extended cellar that houses over 1000 wines, 15 tables in the main house, a conservatory and a private dining room.

Having worked in kitchens since the age of 16, and trained under Marco Pierre White, Daniel is widely regarded as one of the UK's most inventive and talented chefs. His modern British cooking, underpinned by an unmistakably French style, reinvents British classics using the finest local produce. He took part in and won Great British Menu twice with one of the highest scores ever awarded, and has since judged the competition as well as appearing in a number of other TV programmes. But for Daniel, the chefs that have come through the Midsummer kitchen are even more a source of pride than his own achievements; Mark Poynton, Matt Gillan, Elwyn Boyles, Russell Bateman and Tim Allen are just some of those that have gone on to be awarded their own accolades and influenced others in the culinary world.

Current head chef Mark Abbott runs the kitchen these days, having joined the team as chef de partie in 2010. While Daniel has worked on other projects, including his Essex restaurant, Flitch of Bacon, Mark has maintained the kitchen's impeccable standards, and the team at Midsummer have also made a recent return to à la carte menus served alongside the tasting menu. It's a pioneering move for the fine dining establishment and is all about giving the customers more choice, as well as bringing some drama back to the kitchen!

Alongside the £400,000 refurbishment of the kitchen and restaurant, and despite the years of success and sublime food, Daniel Clifford and his team are not about to rest on their laurels anytime soon.

Midsummer House

Midsummer House
CURED MACKEREL

At the restaurant, this dish also incorporates a lime and wasabi gel, pickled radishes, black mouli, daikon cress, pink radish cress, soy jelly, a daikon and lemongrass sorbet and kaffir lime leaf oil.

Preparation time: 5 hours | Cooking time: 1 hour | Serves: 4

Ingredients

For the cured mackerel:

1 mackerel

White wine vinegar

Maldon sea salt

40g XO sauce

5g each of sesame oil, mirin and red miso

10g rice wine vinegar

1g each of salt and sugar

For the mackerel consommé:

10 mackerel carcasses (not heads) and 3 mackerel fillets

1 litre fish stock

3 sticks of lemongrass

Peel of 1 lime

2 sticks of celery

8 egg whites

30g dried katsuobushi

Pinch of Bonito flakes

For the sesame rice:

50g white fondant

50g glucose

1g table salt

20g tahini paste

100g rice

7g each of black and normal sesame seed

For the mackerel purée:

25g sourdough (crusts removed)

75g mackerel

3g salt

7g lemon juice

25g milk

50g double cream

3g rapeseed oil

Method

For the cured mackerel

Start by filleting the mackerel and removing the rib bones. Place skin side down in white wine vinegar for 10 seconds and then remove membrane. Lightly salt on both sides and leave for two hours. Once salted, rinse for 2-3 minutes under running cold water. Dry in a cloth and leave for half an hour. Mix the XO sauce, sesame oil, mirin, miso and the rice wine vinegar in a bowl with the salt and sugar. Once mixed, place in a tray and put the mackerel flesh side down ensuring the skin is not in contact with the marinade. Leave for 1 hour. Once marinated, remove from liquid and put on a separate tray and pat the flesh side with a cloth.

For the mackerel consommé

Put the mackerel carcasses in the oven at 180°c for 12 minutes on full fan and then drain off any fat. Bring the fish stock up to the boil and drop in the carcasses, lemongrass and lime peel. Reduce stock to a gentle simmer and cook for 10 minutes, pass through a sieve and chill. Once chilled remove any scum that has come to the surface, and put in a narrow pan. Blend the mackerel fillets with the celery to get a coarse paste and then combine with the egg whites. Continue to clarify the stock, pass it through muslin and then drop in the dried katsuobushi and Bonito flakes. Leave for 2 minutes, pass again and chill.

For the sesame rice

Put the fondant, glucose and salt in a pan and bring to 150°c. Take off the heat and let it cool for 1 minute, then add the tahini paste ensuring its well incorporated and pour onto on a non-stick mat or tray. Once cool, blend to a fine powder. Heat a pan of oil to 200°c and drop in the rice. Drain and then quickly sieve the powder over the hot puffed rice. Season generously with salt and mix in all the sesame seeds. Transfer to a tray lined with parchment, flatten into one layer, cover in tin foil and then bake at 250°c for 2 minutes. Allow to cool on the tray. Break into clusters.

For the mackerel purée

Soak the sourdough in 5g of water then put everything apart from the milk, cream and rapeseed oil into the blender and blend to a rough paste. Boil the milk and cream together, pour over the ingredients in the blender, blend on full speed until the purée is 75°c and then pass onto ice and emulsify with the rapeseed oil.

To serve

Place the rice clusters in serving dishes and pipe dots of mackerel purée in between. Add 5 or 6 cubes of cured mackerel to each portion and pour over the mackerel consommé. You can garnish with pickled radishes and daikon or pink radish cress as we do in the restaurant if you like.

From India with LOVE

Navadhanya is the one that started it all for Krishna and Arun; a combination of Indian cuisine and refined cooking that takes diners on a journey from the north to the south on the subcontinent.

Cambridge proved to be the perfect place to open their flagship restaurant for cousins Krishna and Arun. They hail from south India, had worked in London, tried out their concept in Gloucester, but the multicultural city with its melting pot of academics, students, families, and professionals welcomed Navadhanya with open arms. Taking the flavours they knew well from childhood and from travelling through India as adults, the ambitious founders of the Indian fine dining experience aimed to deliver authenticity as well as refinement at the restaurant.

Making no secret of the fact they were aiming to feature in the Michelin guide from the very beginning, opened Navadhanya in 2014. The concept has been so successful that it's taken them into 2018 with the accolade they so wanted proudly achieved. Navadhanya's team come from five star and Michelin backgrounds, so they really know how to deliver the "utmost courtesy and hospitality". This includes chef Kamaladasan, who started his culinary journey in Chennai enjoying his mum's cooking. Kamal trained at the Taj Group of Hotels in India, and worked at the Michelin-starred Tamarind Mayfair in London. His creativity and unique style make the chef an integral part of Navadhanya, and the menus are designed in collaboration between himself and the owners.

From lunch, to dinner à la carte or a luxurious seven course tasting menu, Navadhanya's dining options are designed to take guests on a journey through India, from the south to the north through the vibrant and incredibly diverse cuisine of the country. The spices used are imported from India, while the meat is sourced from a local butcher and vegetables are grown locally. Using a fusion of produce from the UK and India means that the menus can be flexible to include the best of the season, so Navadhanya's menus change four times a year to reflect those natural sources. From sweet kulfi to spicy samosas, Navadhanya's take on the unique tastes and textures in Indian food is elegant, delicious, and suffused with the most important ingredient: a genuine love of their culinary heritage and passion for innovating with it from the family team at the restaurant's heart.

Navadhanya
SEA BASS AND CASSAVA WITH AUBERGINE SAUCE

Chef's flavourful sea bass recipe serves the pan-fried fish fillets with mashed cassava. The story behind this dish starts with my mum, who used to make fish in moringa sauce which is still one of my all-time favourites. I decided to make the sea bass in moringa sauce with aubergine and it works very well.

Preparation time: 60 minutes | Cooking time: 30 minutes | Serves: 4

Ingredients

For the sauce:

2 tbsp sunflower oil

½ tsp mustard seeds

½ tsp fenugreek seeds

2 sprigs of curry leaves, picked and stalks discarded

½ tbsp fennel powder

2½cm piece of ginger, peeled and julienned

20g garlic

3 shallots, peeled and sliced

1 tsp chilli powder

½ tsp turmeric powder

1 tbsp ground coriander

Pinch of ground black pepper

4 tomatoes, quartered

4 aubergines, cubed

4 sprigs of moringa, stalks discarded

2 tbsp tomato purée

120ml coconut milk

4 sea bass fillets, skin on and bones removed

To serve:

250g mashed cassava

1 handful of fresh sakura cress

Method

Heat the oil in a pan and put the mustard seeds, fenugreek seeds, curry leaves, fennel powder, ginger, garlic and shallots in to soften. Add the chilli powder, turmeric powder, ground coriander, black pepper, tomatoes, aubergine, moringa, tomato purée, a tablespoon of water and the coconut milk. Bring to the boil and then leave the sauce to simmer for 20 minutes until everything is cooked through.

Place the sea bass fillets a hot pan skin-side down for 2-3 minutes, and then into the sauce to cook over a very low heat for a further 10 minutes.

To serve

When the fish is cooked, the dish is ready to serve. We plate it with a round of mashed cassava in the centre of the dish, topped with the fillet of sea bass, surrounded by the aubergine sauce and garnished with the sakura cress.

Town and GOWN

In the heart of Cambridge, town and gown meet in an iconic building.

The landmark which houses The Oak Bistro today started life as a coaching inn, where many a tired head lay as travellers passed through Cambridge from far-flung places. The Grade II listed building still opens its doors to locals and visitors from around the globe, this time to offer quality food and drink in beautiful surroundings. Philip Newman arrived in Cambridge in 2007, leaving behind his favourite restaurants in leafy North West London, and took a year off work to focus on being a full-time dad while exploring opportunities for opening his own local restaurant.

The first seed was planted when he identified a niche in the market and he was determined to create a place where he and his wife, friends and family would love to go. On finding the perfect venue, an old plaque detailing some of the site's history of the site left Philip in no doubt about what to name his new venture. An ancient oak tree once stood on the site, and the coaching inn had been called The Oak, so it felt only right that the name of the bistro should preserve and continue that heritage.

To reflect this, the decor inside The Oak Bistro is contemporary but classic; understated elegance complemented by the work of local artists, crisp white linen, delicate glassware and fresh flowers. It's the perfect environment to suit talking business over lunch and lunching at leisure. Flickering candlelight and soft music in the evening create the ideal setting for a romantic dinner or that special date night for when you want to impress!

The wines are carefully chosen by Philip, a wine lover who has travelled extensively. Inspired by wine making globally, he has created an eclectic wine list and there are some surprise wines available for even the most discerning wine lover. The menu is classic bistro, with local suppliers providing a Cambridgeshire touch to the work of the head chef and his international team. The confit duck dish is a firm favourite all year round, but was almost dropped from the menu when a brood of ducklings were saved in the restaurant garden…

The Oak Bistro has established itself as a place of celebration, where lots of memories and stories are shared and its staff plan to continue identifying new and fun ways to make dining out a memorable experience. This special Cambridge independent is part of the life story of many locals and visitors to the historic city, who have enjoyed the classic approach to fine food and drink, tailored with that personal touch from those who love it.

The Oak Bistro
CONFIT DUCK LEG

The duck leg from The Oak Bistro is a firm favourite, sourced from one of the finest producers in France. The dish almost left the menu after Philip and his team saved a brood of ducklings left by the mother duck in the restaurant garden. However, due to customer demand it remains on the menu!

Preparation time: 10 minutes, plus 24 hours marinating | Cooking time: 2 hours 10 minutes | Serves: 4

Ingredients

For the duck:

4 duck legs

Salt and pepper

1 clove of garlic, minced

For the mash:

500g red skin potatoes

100ml double cream

50g butter

Salt and pepper

For the braised red cabbage:

200g caster sugar

1 small red cabbage

1 litre red wine

50ml balsamic vinegar

For the rosemary jus:

1 white onion

1 carrot

1 celery stick

Splash of olive oil

1 clove of garlic

1 sprig of rosemary

500ml red wine

1 litre water

50g demi-glace

Method

For the duck

Marinate the legs in the salt, pepper and garlic for 24 hours. When ready, place the legs in a deep-sided baking tray and cover them with water. Cover the tray with foil and then cook the duck for 2 hours at 200°c. After the 2 hours, remove the legs from the liquid and oven bake them for 10 minutes at 200°c.

For the mash

Make the accompaniments while the duck is in the oven. First, peel and then boil the potatoes for 30 minutes. Drain the potatoes when tender and then mash in the cream, butter, salt and pepper to create a smooth texture.

For the braised red cabbage

Caramelise the sugar in a wide pan, and then add the cabbage and let it sweat. Keep the pan on a medium heat to let any liquid steam off. Add the wine and vinegar, then leave to simmer for 30 minutes on a low heat. Keep warm until ready to serve.

For the rosemary jus

Finely chop the onion, carrot and celery. Fry the vegetables and garlic in olive oil on a gentle heat until soft. Add the rosemary and the wine, then let it simmer and reduce for about 10 minutes. Add a litre of water and the demi-glace, simmer for another 10 minutes stirring all the time, and then let the jus reduce to the required consistency.

To serve

Serve the duck leg with a generous helping of creamy mash, braised red cabbage and rosemary jus.

It's all Greek TO ME

Fresh food and family time – these are the simple but crucial ingredients that make The Olive Grove's award-winning authentic Greek food and drink so appealing.

Francesca and George Kontakos opened The Olive Grove in 2013 to bring the staples of their Greek upbringing – flavoursome, freshly prepared food enjoyed with family – to Cambridge. With a background in hospitality and a culinary heritage they are very proud of, the husband and wife team have introduced the delights of authentic Greek dishes to an audience who have loved the laid-back, plentiful and sharing-focused dining experience at the restaurant.

Classic Greek tavern food is relatively well-known in the UK, but The Olive Grove has a whole host of recipes – some passed down through Francesca and George's families, some developed with their head chef Nikos Krassas – that open up new avenues of flavour for customers. They don't like to do things the same way as everyone else, and are passionate about filling the gap people in the UK don't even know they're missing for really fresh food that represents Greek cuisine as it is being cooked today.

Mezze is the most important element of any Greek meal, which goes hand in hand with ordering lots of plates to share with friends and family. Francesca and George really encourage this convivial way of eating and drinking together; children are always welcome in the restaurant and the atmosphere is all about allowing people to feel comfortable and at home, including staying as long as they like because typically, Greek meals can last up to six hours!

The freshest ingredients available, sourced locally and sustainably as much as possible, form the backbone of chef Nikos' kitchen. His menu changes with the seasons – except for firm favourites such as the moussaka and the mouth-watering selection of grilled food – and makes the most of the exceptional flavour that comes from the best produce. Because everything is cooked to order, it's easily adapted for those with dietary requirements too, and vegetarian, vegan and gluten-free food is already integral to the balance of taste and nutrition in Greek food, so whether your dish is based around fresh fish, meat, or vegetables it will be made with a genuine love of this way of cooking.

Being family-run means that The Olive Grove offers something unique; Francesca and George have infused everything from the welcome to the predominantly Greek wine list with their ethos and the personal connection they have to the food they grew up with. It's not just about eating and drinking, but embracing a way of being together and savouring simple meals, fresh from the kitchen and straight from the heart of Greece and its inspiring culinary style.

The Olive Grove
MOUSSAKA

An all-time Greek classic that's integral to Greek gastronomy, which became popular in the 20th century thanks to the Greek chef Nikó Tselementés. Even today, moussaka is the most renowned Greek dish in the world. Although much preparation is needed, the end result is mouth-wateringly good!

Preparation time: 40 minutes | Cooking time: approx. 1½ hours | Serves: 4-6

Ingredients

For the vegetables:

3 large potatoes

3 aubergines

50ml white vinegar

150g plain flour

Oil for deep frying

For the bolognese:

1 small carrot

1 small leek

1 large red onion

2 cloves of garlic

1kg beef mince (20% fat)

50ml extra-virgin olive oil

150g tomato purée

100ml water

½ tsp ground cinnamon

1 bay leaf

½ tsp oregano

Salt and pepper, to taste

For the béchamel:

2 litres full-fat fresh milk

1 tsp nutmeg

Salt and pepper, to taste

150g salted butter

200g plain flour

Method

For the vegetables

Peel and slice the potatoes into rings approximately 1cm thick. Keep the skin on the aubergines and slice them the same size. Place the aubergine slices in a large bowl and cover with cold water and the white vinegar. This is to take away the bitter taste from the aubergines; they need to soak for 20 minutes. Deep fry the potatoes at 120°c until they are soft and golden in colour. Dust the aubergines with plain flour and fry at 180°c until they are soft on the inside but crispy on the outside. Place all the potato and aubergine slices on kitchen towel to soak up excess oil.

For the bolognese

Finely chop the carrot, leek, onion and garlic. Add the beef mince to a saucepan with the olive oil on a medium heat until it is cooked through. Add the chopped vegetables and sauté for 5 minutes, then add the tomato purée, all the seasonings and 100ml of water. Leave the bolognese to simmer on a low heat for 20 minutes until all the liquid has evaporated.

For the béchamel

Warm the milk in a saucepan on a low heat with the nutmeg, salt and pepper. Do not bring to boil. In a separate saucepan, melt the butter and slowly add the flour while consistently stirring until the roux becomes golden in colour. Add the roux to the milk and continue stirring it until the béchamel is thick.

To build the moussaka

You will need a 5cm deep baking tray. Start by adding three tablespoons of bolognese sauce to the tray, then a layer of potatoes seasoned with salt and pepper, then a layer of cooked aubergine. Add the remaining bolognese, then the béchamel sauce. Bake the moussaka at 180°c in a preheated oven for 45 minutes.

The Olive Grove
BARBOUNI AND SKORDALIA

A modern day Greek dish inspired by the past! Fresh red mullet, garlic, fresh thyme and white wine are four characteristics of the dish, which transports you with every bite to a Greek idyll of blue seas and sunsets.

Preparation time: 10 minutes | Cooking time: 30 minutes | Serves: 1

Ingredients

For the barbouni:

2 fillets of red mullet

2 tbsp extra-virgin olive oil

100g plain flour

Salt and pepper

2 spring onions, finely chopped

1 clove of garlic, grated

2 cherry tomatoes, quartered

2 sprigs of fresh thyme

100ml Greek white wine (preferably retsina)

80g cold salted butter, cubed

1 tbsp fresh lemon juice

1 tsp fresh dill, finely chopped

For the skordalia:

1 large potato

40g butter

2 cloves of garlic, grated

Salt and pepper

2 tbsp double cream

Method

For the barbouni

Ensure that the mullet is clean and all the scales and bones have been removed. Place a frying pan on a medium to high heat and add the olive oil to it. Dust the fish fillets with flour lightly seasoned with salt and pepper and then place them in a frying pan skin side down. Press the fillet down at first so that it doesn't curl. Leave to cook for 3 minutes on a medium heat, turning once to ensure it cooks through evenly. Add the spring onions, garlic, cherry tomatoes and fresh thyme. Add the wine and flambé. Once the flames die out take the pan off the heat and add the butter and lemon juice. Garnish with the fresh dill.

For the skordalia

Boil the potato until soft and then mash. Melt the butter in a saucepan on a low heat. Add the garlic and mashed potato to the butter with salt and pepper to taste, and then stir in the double cream to finish.

To serve

Put a generous helping of skordalia on the plate and lay the red mullet fillet on top.

The Olive Grove
TYROKAFTERI

This is now one of the most popular side dishes in Greek cuisine that varies from village to village and city to city. You can find it made with green peppers, florina peppers, or even without peppers. The most important thing is that it's a tasty dip, and can be served with fresh bread or warm Greek pitta, but is also a great accompaniment for grilled meat or even fresh fish.

Preparation time: 5 minutes | Serves: 2

Ingredients

200g feta

1 spring onion

3 tbsp olive oil

1 small red chilli

1 tsp dried oregano

1 florina pepper

2 tbsp white vinegar

Method

Add all the ingredients except for the feta cheese to a blender and blend to combine everything. Grate the feta cheese in a separate bowl. Fold all the ingredients together. Serve with warm pitta bread.

Chef's tip

The consistency of this dip must not be watery. Depending on how fresh the feta cheese is, you might need to add a little more feta.

From Aphrodite to BLIGHTY

OliveOlive makes the finest olive oils, direct from the owner's family farm, and authentic handmade halloumi available to anyone with a taste for the best of Cypriot produce.

Husband and wife Rob and Pam were lucky enough to enjoy the purest olives and oils straight from the source, Pam's family farm in Cyprus, long before they dreamt of starting their own business.

The idea came when cooking with or serving the olive oil for their friends; they got so many compliments about how good it was, and questions about where it came from, they decided to make the product more widely available in the UK and OliveOlive was born.

Their secret is in sticking to the traditional way their olives are handpicked, pressed and bottled. The journey of the olives can be traced from tree to bottle. Nothing is added, nothing is taken away; put simply, it's 100% olive juice.

Since then Rob and Pam have diversified to highlight other authentic Cypriot products, such as their own range of fused olive oils. Unlike the infused varieties that you find in most supermarkets, they produce their flavoured fused oils by pressing fresh basil, chilli or garlic with the olives, instead of steeping them in the finished oil; this imparts a much cleaner, more intense flavour.

Completing the mouth-watering trio is their village-style halloumi. This is handmade in the traditional method by the Stephani family of professional cheese makers, who also happen to be good friends of Rob and Pam. The halloumi is produced with pure goat's milk, which makes it flavourful as well as producing a denser and more satisfying texture, and uses vegetable rennet, meaning vegetarians can enjoy their halloumi too. It also carries a 'best in Cyprus' award; though more importantly Rob's mother-in-law recommends it, and as Rob says; you don't argue with your Greek mother-in-law!

Rob and Pam are closely involved in every aspect of their business. They regularly go to Cyprus to help with the olive harvest and source new products, then distribute these back home through food festivals, farmers' markets, fine food stores and award-winning restaurants, as well as selling them direct online. Their website offers everyone the chance to buy OliveOlive products and gifts from anywhere in the UK; Rob and Pam have plenty of regular customers that they have never met, but who keep coming back for more!

Customers who stock up on halloumi and oils at their stall always tell them how glad they are that OliveOlive offer an authentic taste of Cyprus here in the UK and after tasting the real thing, they just cannot go back to bland supermarket versions.

Their celebrity clients include Cypriot-born entrepreneur Theo Paphitis and Michelin-starred chef Galton Blackiston from Morston Hall in Norfolk.

OliveOlive
STUFF THAT! CHICKEN WITH EASY PESTO

Wondering what to do for tea tonight? Try one of our favourites: chicken thighs stuffed with halloumi cheese and wrapped in streaky bacon, then topped with a quick and easy pesto.

Preparation time: 10 minutes | Cooking time: approx. 1 hour | Serves 4

Ingredients

For the chicken:

1 red and 1 yellow pepper, chopped into medium chunks

1 courgette, sliced thinly

1 red onion, sliced

1 leek, chopped into chunky discs

About 20 cherry tomatoes

2 cloves of garlic, grated or crushed

2 tbsp OliveOlive Garlic Fused Olive Oil

Salt and pepper

½ block of the finest halloumi cheese known to mankind (we suggest ours)

8 boneless and skinless chicken thighs

16 rashers smoked streaky bacon

For the pesto:

30g fresh basil leaves

2 cloves of garlic, grated or crushed

1 lemon, juiced

Salt and pepper

3 tbsp of the finest extra-virgin olive oil known to mankind (we suggest ours)

Method

For the chicken

Preheat the oven to 240°c (220°c for a fan oven) and place the prepared vegetables and garlic into a roasting dish. Drizzle with garlic olive oil and season (don't go overboard with the salt though; there is plenty of salt already in the bacon and halloumi). Slice the halloumi into long thick chunks and place inside the fold of the chicken thighs. Roll up and wrap with bacon; use two rashers per thigh. Place the stuffed and wrapped chicken thighs on the bed of vegetables and cover the whole dish with foil. Place in the oven for 45 minutes and check every 15 minutes, stirring the veg regularly. After 45 minutes of cooking, remove the foil and roast uncovered for a further 15 minutes.

For the pesto

Make the pesto while the chicken and vegetables are roasting. Place all the ingredients except the olive oil into a food processor. Pour in the olive oil while blitzing until the required consistency is reached. Pour over the cooked chicken as desired and enjoy!

Something Old, Something NEW

Opening in 2018 after a lavish and loving reinvention, Parker's Tavern makes the most of Cambridge's heritage and the best of modern innovation in design, architecture, food and drink.

University Arms, a historic Cambridge hotel that first opened in 1834 and has been restored following an 80 million pound investment, is now home to Parker's Tavern, a quintessentially British brasserie that celebrates feasting and the city that inspires it in equal measure. Tristan Welch is the chef director, and the realisation of this landmark project in his career has been a homecoming for him in more ways than one. Having grown up in Cambridge, Tristan has returned with a wealth of experience – gained from his travels across the world and his training in the best European kitchens alongside Gary Rhodes, Michel Roux Jr. and Gordon Ramsay – to put good unpretentious British food back on the menu.

Tristan's philosophy starts with letting Mother Nature decide what to put on the plate. What's in season around him becomes the star of the show, whether that's local asparagus at the peak of its brief season or sashimi made with fish from British waters. Bringing these skills back into the kitchen is really important to Tristan; his team prepare whole animals for the fish and meat section, temper chocolate for the handmade bonbons in a chocolate tempering room, and make their own ice cream to be enjoyed on Parker's Piece in summertime. His food aims to reflect the beauty, intelligence and ambition of Cambridge, with a whimsical touch that nods to his own flamboyance and great passion for the dishes he creates.

This ethos has been shared and complemented by everyone contributing to the brasserie's renaissance. Swedish designer Martin Brudnizki has mingled the convivial feel of college halls with luxurious fabrics and modern yet elegant style that emphasises the original features – magnificent fireplaces, stained glass windows – amidst relaxed and informal fun. The spaces that have been brought back to life include a ballroom and dining room where dinners and lunches will be served, a bar featuring botanical-inspired cocktails and treasures from the impressive wine cellar, and a library where afternoon teas pay homage to the city's great wordsmiths.

Above all, Tristan wants to conjure up a "delicious taste of Cambridge" in this very special setting. His own food memories, the diversity of its people, walks along the River Cam: the city feeds the creative process he has undertaken, during which culinary delights such as Fidget Pie, Duke of Cambridge Tart, Burnt Cream and good old 'spag bol' have enjoyed his interpretation. A perfect marriage of homely and luxurious, Parker's Tavern will be an integral part of Cambridge for many more years to come.

Parker's Tavern
CHICKEN TIKKA MASALA PIE

Chef director Tristan Welch has a tip; 'Before you start this recipe, I have to warn you it is best made a day in advance.'

Preparation time: 90 minutes, plus marinating | Cooking time: 30 minutes | Serves 8

Ingredients

1 whole chicken

For the marinade:

4 tsp salt

1 tsp hot chilli powder and ground coriander each

3cm fresh ginger

3 cloves of garlic

3 tbsp Greek yoghurt

2 tsp fenugreek

2 tbsp mustard oil

½ pepper and onion, chopped

1 tomato, chopped

For the masala sauce:

1 onion, finely chopped

3 cloves of garlic, crushed

6cm of fresh ginger, chopped

1 knob of butter

1 cinnamon stick

3 green cardamom pods

1 tsp turmeric and chilli powder each

2 bay leaves

3 cloves

2 tsp coriander and cumin seeds each

1 can tinned tomatoes, blended

4 tbsp cashew nuts, blended

1 tsp salt

300ml double cream

For the shortcrust pastry:

150g plain flour

75g butter, cubed

2-3 tbsp cold water

Pinch of salt

To finish:

1 egg

Cumin seeds

Method

For the marinade

Toast the spices in a pan over a low heat until you can smell the fragrance, then add this to the remaining marinade ingredients and blend into a paste. Put the marinade in a plastic bag with the chicken, ensuring it's well covered, and place in the fridge overnight, allowing the flavours to infuse. Roast the chicken at 190°c for an hour and allow to rest. Pick the chicken meat off the bone in thumb-sized pieces and set to one side.

For the masala sauce

Slowly fry the onion, ginger, garlic and spices in butter for a couple of minutes. Blend the tinned tomatoes and cashew nuts until smooth, then add this to the onion and spices. Cook for a further 20 minutes. Once cooked, add the cream and bring to the boil, then add the chicken meat. Test for seasoning, then fill a pie dish with the mixture and allow to cool.

For the shortcrust pastry

Meanwhile, place the flour, salt and butter in a bowl and rub together using your fingertips until it resembles breadcrumbs. Ensure there are no large lumps of butter remaining. Gradually stir in just enough of the cold water to bind the dough together, then roll it to roughly 5mm thick. Cover and chill for 20 minutes.

To finish

Place the pastry on top of the pie dish, cutting away any excess pastry. Pinch the edges of the pastry with your thumb and finger to seal the pastry to the dish. Brush with the egg, add a sprinkle of cumin seeds, and bake at 180°c for half an hour.

Best of BOTH

In 2013, an empty Grade Two listed building in the heart of Cambridge provided the perfect spot for the realisation of a dream involving great food and great beer...

Who could resist the pairing of charcoal-grilled meat and a cold beer, or a Scotch egg hot from the fryer accompanied by a refreshing G&T? The double passions of founders Rich and Benny are in mouth-watering evidence at their first Pint Shop on Cambridge's Peas Hill. Their idea was to establish a place where all would be welcome to enjoy a favourite drink, a delicious meal, or ideally both in equal measure! The inspiration is British classics, but the menus keep stodgy puds and overdone veg at arm's length, instead taking an old favourite like chicken and chips and cooking the beer-brined bird on a spit roast over hot coals for a real treat with a twist.

Starting with simple concepts and turning them into standout food and drink is Pint Shop's speciality. It's especially important to Rich and Benny that one doesn't come at the expense of the other. Emphasis on the beer and gin side of the venture stems from the advent of 1830s beer houses, which followed a spate of mostly illegal gin-drinking by those who couldn't afford the highly-taxed alternatives. Thankfully, things have improved since then and people from all walks of life are happily received at Pint Shop whatever their tipple

of choice. The staff are ready and waiting to match any drink with a dish – think dry-aged steaks, flatbread kebabs, or gin-cured sea trout – that's sure to tickle your taste buds.

Rich and Benny continue to guarantee that the staff have as much personality and pizazz as the food to create an all-round experience for each guest. Pint Shop people pride themselves on the knowledge they can accumulate and pass on to customers about the food and drink they offer. This approach goes hand in hand with building good relationships with suppliers and other local businesses, especially Cambridgeshire breweries with whom the team can collaborate and learn from, though Jack's Gelato has proved a fruitful partner too! Rich and Benny have remained at the heart of the business since they established it, and their ethos has embedded Pint Shop in the growing food community across the city.

The industrial charm of the 1830s venue reflects the honest approach of the founders and the simplicity of what they want to achieve: a warm, homely atmosphere that lets the genuine love of food and drink shine through in all its glory.

Pint Shop
BRAISED AND CHARRED PORK CHEEKS AND BLACK PUDDING HASH

This dish was created by our lovely head chef Mikey from our sister Pint Shop in Oxford. "In winter you want something rich and super satisfying, and the pig cheeks deliver that as they have done a lot of work and with that comes deep flavour". We have paired them simply with a hash as this allows the strong flavours of the cheek to stand out, and then added a touch of black pudding magic for a pleasant surprise when you cut into it.

Preparation time: 20 minutes | Cooking time: approx. 3½ hours | Serves 6

Ingredients

12 cheeks (about 500g) pork cheeks, ask your butchers to trim the sinew

Pinch of salt

Drizzle of rapeseed oil

2 sticks of celery, washed and cut into 2cm angled slices

2 small white onions, peeled and cut into wedges

2 carrots, peeled and cut into 2cm angled slices

1 leek, green tops sliced off and sliced into 2cm angled slices

250ml dry classic cider (we use Oakham's)

500ml chicken stock (homemade, or a stock pot is fine)

3 juniper berries, lightly crushed

4 allspice berries

10 black peppercorns

2 bay leaves

Small tied bunch of thyme

1 star anise

4 cloves

2 cardamom pods, gently crushed

For the black pudding hash:

1½kg potatoes, peeled

1 whole egg

10g table salt

3g black pepper

100g black pudding, roughly crumbled

2g ground allspice

50-100g salted butter

Method

Preheat a griddle pan until it's lightly smoking. Lightly salt the cheeks and toss in a drop of rapeseed oil. Place them onto the griddle and cook for 4-5 minutes on each side to get some nice grill marks. Set to one side. Toss the vegetables in a little rapeseed oil, season them with salt and pepper, and then grill the celery, onions, carrots and leeks for 4-5 minutes on each side in the same pan until they are nicely charred.

Put all the ingredients, including the spices, in a heavy casserole dish and add salt and pepper to taste (keep the seasoning light at this point). Cover with baking paper, pop the lid on and place the dish into the oven. Cook at 150°c for 2 to 2 and a half hours until the cheeks are meltingly tender. Remove from the oven and allow the cheeks to cool in the liquor. Once cool, remove the cheeks and vegetables and put to one side. Place the pan back onto the hob and bring the liquor to a simmer. Reduce by one quarter, check the seasoning and then leave to cool again. When the hash is ready, warm the cheeks and the veggies in the reduced liquor.

For the black pudding hash

Immerse the potatoes (keep them whole) in cold water and bring to the boil for 1 minute. Lift out and leave to cool down until you can just handle them. Grate the potato and discard any excess water. Beat the egg and mix in the salt and pepper. Thoroughly mix the seasoned egg into the grated potato. Take a 20-25cm frying pan (ideally non-stick) and rub with butter. Place half of the potato mix into the frying pan to cover the bottom. Scatter over the black pudding and ground allspice then cover that with the final half of the potato mix. Heat the pan on the hob over a medium flame. The hash should be a lovely golden brown underneath before you turn it over. To turn the hash over in one go, give the edge a little nudge with a fish slice to loosen it, then place a plate on top and turn the hash out. Slide back into the pan with a little more butter and repeat the cooking process on the other side. Finish cooking the hash in a 180°c oven for 5-8 minutes or until crispy.

Keeping it in THE FAMILY

Continuing a family legacy that began 150 years ago, Prana is proud to serve authentic Indian food that combines tradition with reinvention.

Kobir owns and runs Prana, the award-winning Indian restaurant on Cambridge's Mill Road, bringing his own and his family's expertise to the distinctive dining experience he has created. Prana draws on a culinary heritage that began with Kobir's great-great grandfather, who opened a classic Indian tea bar in Bangladesh, and has been passed down through generations of restaurateurs. Kobir's uncle was the first to open a restaurant in the UK, and many of Prana's dishes are now based on his original menu. Popular traditional options are included alongside new creations that reflect modern Indian cooking as well as Kobir's individual approach to the cuisine he grew up with.

His ethos has developed around a firm commitment to the very freshest and best quality ingredients; the restaurant buys vegetables on a daily basis and all the spices used are ground and blended in the kitchen rather than bought in pre-prepared, making the flavours of each dish really distinct. The differences in Prana's style of cooking result in beautifully plated dishes, vibrant with the natural colours of fresh sauces that don't rely on a typical fried spice and tomato base. Served with naan made to a vegan recipe (which produces a much lighter, flavoursome accompaniment) Prana's menu is designed to have a wide appeal, as well as tasting amazing!

To complement the love and care that goes into his food, it's important to Kobir that the restaurant itself is presented just as attractively. Traditional colours and decorative touches, real roses on each table, and even ironed tablecloths stem from attention to detail instilled in him by growing up amidst his family's hospitality business. In 2017, Prana was declared England's Restaurant of the Year at the English Curry Awards, the business' seventh award to date and the biggest so far in a growing list of achievements.

From childhood memories of helping to wash up in the family restaurant, stood on buckets to reach the sink, to running a successful restaurant of his own with numerous accolades to its name, Kobir has channelled his passion for Indian dining to put his own spin on the history that has shaped Prana's food and concept. He says that "pushing the boundaries of how Indian restaurants should be run" is part of his drive to be the best, and loves being able to provide Cambridge with a first-class experience of the depth and breadth of Indian cuisine.

Prana Indian Restaurant

KHADAM PHOOL

This tasty recipe is quick and easy; the combination of minced lamb and spicy mashed potatoes coated with breadcrumbs and deep fried is really moreish! A family favourite loved by kids and adults alike at our restaurant.

Preparation time: 15 minutes | Cooking time: 15 minutes | Serves: 2-3

Ingredients

Vegetable oil, to fry

1 onion, finely chopped

100g lamb mince

Salt and pepper

Pinch of turmeric

Pinch of garam masala

650g mashed potato

Small bunch of coriander, freshly chopped

115g chickpea (gram) flour

1 egg, beaten with a little salt and pepper

100-200g dry breadcrumbs

A few green chillies, finely chopped to garnish (optional)

Method

Heat a pan with a little vegetable oil. Add the onion, mince, a pinch of salt, turmeric, and garam masala. Stir-fry until the onion and lamb are cooked through, and then allow to cool. Mix in the mashed potato and coriander until well combined, and then add the gram flour and fold through.

Place the beaten egg and breadcrumbs in two separate bowls. Take a handful of the potato and meat mixture, shape it into a ball, dip it into the egg and then into the breadcrumbs. Heat the remaining vegetable oil in a small pan, over a medium-high heat. Deep fry the coated potato and lamb balls in small batches until evenly browned, turning once. Place them on a plate lined with kitchen towel to cool and let excess oil drain off.

To serve

When all the balls are fried, plate with your preference of salad and dipping sauce or chutney, and serve while still hot.

Be Outside
THE BOX

Prévost is the culmination of Lee Clarke's experiences as a chef in the UK's top kitchens, and offers fine dining with a difference...

Lee Clarke learnt his trade working at The Ivy, Harvey Nichols and Marco Pierre White's restaurants, but it was during his time at Ickworth Hotel in Bury St. Edmunds – much closer to home for the Cambridgeshire-born chef – that he really started to develop his own style of cooking. The grounds provided lots of opportunities for foraging, the estate keeper helped with catching rabbit and hare for the menu, and the lamb came from farms on the edges of the estate. Under Lee's guidance as head chef, the hotel's restaurant gained and held two AA rosettes.

Following that success, Lee was head chef at Clarkes in Peterborough, a restaurant he had been involved in since its opening, and has been at the heart of for six years. The ambition to create his own food was still driving him forward though, which led to the conception of Prévost. As Lee says, "it's still my main ambition to have the first Michelin-starred restaurant in Peterborough and I could not see it happening if I was not the owner. You can only suggest and push things so far, I understand that." With free reign to offer his own take on fine dining, Lee has put together an experience that combines bold flavours without the boundaries, and an atmosphere that aims to welcome guests warmly without the formalities.

When it comes to the food, there's a big emphasis on home-grown and locally sourced ingredients at Prévost. The kitchen works with produce from its own allotment, from carrots and beetroot to Swiss chard and strawberries. Prévost even produces its own honey, and what the team don't grow they source from local suppliers where possible. It's always been about serving seasonal food; the dedication to nurturing ingredients from plot to plate really shows, not only in how beautiful the food looks on the plate, but in how it tastes.

The restaurant offers a set three course lunch and dinner menu, as well as five and nine course tasting menus. This can be accompanied by an extensive wine list to enjoy by the glass or as a flight, as well as artisan ales and imaginative twists on classic cocktails from the bar. With more vegetarian and vegan options than ever before, Lee says, "offering decent alternatives means we can accommodate anyone with dietary differences so nobody feels they're missing out." The ethos of not being boxed in permeates Prévost, driven by Lee and his passion for introducing a new culinary experience to Cambridgeshire for everyone to sample.

Prévost
NORFOLK QUAIL AND QUAIL SCOTCH EGG

I love quail, and it goes well with just about any garnish, from haricot blanc and carrots in the winter to Jersey potatoes, asparagus and wild garlic in spring time.

Preparation time: 1 hour | Cooking time: 1 hour | Serves: 4

Ingredients

For the quail:

4 large quail

250ml oil

2 sprigs of thyme

3 cloves of garlic

Salt and pepper

Knob of butter

For the quail Scotch egg:

200g sausage meat

6 fresh sage leaves, finely chopped

4 quail's eggs

3 eggs

150ml milk

Flour

Breadcrumbs

For the quail sherry sauce:

Trimmings from quail

1 onion, finely chopped

2 cloves of garlic, finely chopped

2 fresh tomatoes, finely chopped

2 sticks of celery, finely chopped

100ml sherry

400ml brown chicken stock

Knob of butter

Few drops of sherry vinegar

Method

For the quail

Ask your butcher to prepare the quail, removing the legs and breasts from each but keeping all the trimmings for stock. Infuse the oil by placing the thyme and garlic into it and put in a roasting tray with the quail legs. Cook the legs at 90°c for 1 hour and then remove from the heat and leave to cool. Cook the quail breasts in a frying pan with a drizzle of the oil used to cook the legs, evenly colouring the whole breast until it starts to turn golden brown. After the skin starts to colour, season with salt and pepper and add a generous helping of butter, basting the quail until the skin is golden brown. Remove from the heat and allow to rest for 5 minutes.

For the quail Scotch egg

Mix the sausage meat and sage together. Boil the eggs for 2 minutes and 30 seconds, refresh in iced water, then peel. Take a quarter of the sausage meat and shape it into an even disk. Place a quail egg in the centre and wrap the sausage meat around the egg until it covers the egg and is roughly the size of a golf ball. Repeat with all four eggs.

Whisk the eggs thoroughly with the milk. To coat the Scotch egg, roll the balls in flour until the sausage meat is covered. Remove any excess flour, then roll in the egg mixture until you have an even coating. Lastly, roll in breadcrumbs so the whole surface of the Scotch egg is covered. When ready to serve, deep fry the Scotch eggs at 180°c for 2 minutes. They should be evenly golden brown and the yolk still runny.

For the quail sherry sauce

Fry the trimmings in a pan with the onion, garlic, tomatoes and celery until the vegetables are soft and translucent. Add the sherry and reduce until nearly gone, then add the chicken stock and simmer until reduced to a quarter of the original volume. Pass through a fine mesh sieve and then whisk in a knob of butter and 3-4 drops of sherry vinegar. Ideally, the sauce should coat the back of a spoon evenly and not be too thick or lumpy.

To finish

At Prévost, we serve the quail, Scotch egg and sauce with some fresh asparagus, Jersey Royal new potatoes, wild garlic – which we sweat down with chopped shallots and a knob of butter – and roasted baby leeks.

Provenance is  KEY

The small team behind Provenance Kitchen have not only taken restaurant-standard food and recreated it on the move, they've done it all with wood and coal-fired cooking.

Professional chef Greg Proud and his partner Kate Holden have taken their catering venture all over Cambridge for a few years now, on a day-to-day adventure in innovative and delicious food. The concept behind the cuisine at Provenance Kitchen is to take food you would normally expect to find in a restaurant to wherever people wish it to be. The couple's converted original 1967 Airstream trailer makes this possible and a lot of fun, having been kitted out with wood-fired ovens and Japanese coal-fired braziers which Greg and his sous chef James cook all the food in or on.

The menus, which are updated monthly, stem from seasonal produce and draw on Greg's high-end industry experience to find wonderfully unique and tasty ways of using it. Modern British describes the general leaning but flavours from all over the world sit beautifully alongside fish, meat and vegetables that come about as directly from producer to plate as it gets. Provenance Kitchen now also has its own taco truck – a former horsebox – to widen the repertoire of local, sustainable and ethical options for all occasions.

The Airstream's calendar is as varied as it is eclectic. Greg and Kate often work with pubs and similar venues in Cambridge that don't have kitchen space to put on catered events, and enjoy collaborations with local independents like Cambridge Distillery for an evening of fine gin and fine food once a month. Private parties and weddings can be even more bespoke affairs, with individuals and couples able to choose up to four courses all cooked and served by the Provenance team. Kate explains that providing dining experiences anyone can enjoy – dietary and lifestyle requirements included – is a big consideration for events too. "To us, food is completely inclusive and everyone should be catered for."

Having set themselves apart with their distinctive mobile kitchens and methods of cooking, it's onwards and upwards for the catering pioneers. Recognition of their efforts, both for flavour and ethos, has come in the form of accolades from Cambridge Sustainable Food and The Observer Food Monthly. Based on a farm and inspired by local suppliers, Provenance Kitchen lets the food speak for itself; when you see and taste what can be created with great fresh ingredients and an open flame, you'll absolutely understand why!

CHARRED OCTOPUS WITH SMOKED AUBERGINE AND CHICKPEAS

This recipe is a firm favourite with chef Greg, who likes the dish because it's flexible enough to be served as a starter or a main course. The unusual, bold flavours marry really well together and it's a great way of trying octopus for the first time.

Preparation time: 15 minutes | Cooking time: approx. 4½ hours | Serves 6-8

Ingredients

2kg octopus, frozen and then defrosted (this will help to tenderise it)

1 orange, quartered

1 lemon, halved

1 tsp coriander seeds

1 tsp black peppercorns

½ tsp dried chilli flakes

3-4 sprigs of thyme

1 tin of chickpeas, drained

1 tbsp harissa

For the smoked aubergine:

2 aubergines

1 lemon, zested and juiced

1 clove of garlic, crushed

½ tsp Maldon sea salt

2 tbsp extra-virgin olive oil

⅛ tsp shichimi togarashi

1 tbsp coriander, chopped

To serve:

Shaved radish

Fennel tops

Method

Place the octopus, orange, lemon, coriander seeds, black peppercorns, dried chilli flakes and thyme into a deep roasting tray and cook for 1 hour in the oven at 160°c. After this time, cover the tray with parchment paper and foil. You don't need to add any liquid or salt as the octopus will cook in its natural juices. Cook for a further 3 hours at 150°c until tender. Reserve 150ml of cooking liquid and add the chickpeas and harissa to it. Taste to check the seasoning.

For the smoked aubergine

Cook the aubergines whole over hot wood coals (or directly over a gas flame using tongs) until charred, and then place them in the oven at 160°c for 20-30 minutes until soft. Leave to rest until the aubergines are at room temperature, then remove the charred skin and place the rest of the aubergine in a food processor. Add the rest of the ingredients to the aubergines and blend until silky smooth.

To serve

Cut the octopus tentacles off the body and char over hot coals on a grill or in a hot cast iron pan. Heat up the chickpea mixture. Spoon the aubergine purée onto the plate, top with chickpeas, add the octopus and dress with some of the leftover cooking liquid. Finish with shaved radish, fennel and a squeeze of lemon juice.

The Proof is in THE PUDDINI

Alex and Lindsay's love of food has been the foundation for their flourishing catering business, providing venues and party-goers across Cambridgeshire with dining experiences whose reputation for fantastic quality and flavour precedes them.

The founders and owners of Puddini, Lindsay Scrivener and Alex Harris, have had a "whirlwind" few years developing a new direction for their young business, which started life as a small deli. Such was the popularity of and demand for the food they were creating that the couple decided to focus solely on the catering side of things. This has gone from strength to strength and Puddini is now in the midst of exciting times, with a rebrand and new website underway to ring in the changes.

Alex is a trained chef – he worked under Richard Stokes, formerly of The Three Horseshoes in Madingley, for 15 years – and found a love for Italianate cuisine through catering as well as his previous experience at the River Café in London. He and Lindsay met while working on opposite sides of the pass in a restaurant, but both wanted to follow bigger ambitions, so when a deli came up to let in the village it was all or nothing. The same premises now provide Puddini with a tasting room and office to accommodate the wide range of individuals and businesses that Alex and Lindsay work with today. From weddings to university events and parties to intimate gatherings, their catering calendar is as full as it is eclectic. Having also welcomed their first baby since they became full-time caterers, the couple "couldn't be happier" about the way their concept has taken off.

With two more full-timers, Ashleigh and Ian, and a "wonderful" bank of events staff, Puddini is growing faster than its proud parents ever anticipated. Reviewing the menus regularly as a team while remaining open to clients' ideas means that the food stays up to the minute and can always be personalised. The current street food craze has been really fun to work with, says Lindsay, and they have also got to grips with lots of vegan dishes recently. Seasonality is very much taken into account too, helped by the strong relationships the pair has built up with nearby suppliers, including Longhorn, a butcher just four miles down the road, and Bushel Box for fruit grown on site.

Lindsay and Alex have used everything they've learned to develop a clear vision of exactly what they want to do more of. The whole ethos at Puddini is suffused with their genuine love for the dining experiences they provide, and they are raring to go in this next chapter of food and fun!

Puddini
CHARGRILLED RUMP OF LAMB AND STUFFED COURGETTE FLOWERS

This recipe is one of our favourites and really says summer for us! Courgette flowers are often discarded, but they are absolutely delicious served in this way. We recommend creating this dish in the summer months, when courgettes are in season and their flowers are much easier to source.

Preparation time: 40 minutes, plus 1 – 12 hours marinating | Cooking time: 30 minutes | Serves 6

Ingredients

2x 225g lamb rumps

For the marinade:

1 lemon, roughly chopped

Few sprigs each of mint and rosemary, leaves picked

2 cloves of garlic, peeled

200ml vegetable oil

For the dressing:

1 large red chilli, deseeded and finely chopped

Handful of fresh mint, finely chopped

3 tsp white wine vinegar

100ml extra virgin olive oil

For the vignole:

6 slices of pancetta, diced

Extra virgin olive oil

1 red onion, peeled and finely sliced

4 cloves of garlic, finely chopped

1 bunch of asparagus, ends removed

400g tin of artichoke hearts, drained and quartered

500g each of shelled broad beans and peas

A large handful of fresh mint, leaves picked and finely chopped

A small handful of flat leaf parsley, leaves picked and finely chopped

Maldon sea salt and black pepper

For the stuffed courgette flowers:

150g ricotta

1 lemon, zested

Pinch of chilli flakes

6 basil leaves, roughly chopped

6 courgette flowers, stalks trimmed

200g self-raising flour

400ml sparkling water

Method

For the lamb and marinade

In a food processor, blitz all the ingredients together and then pour the marinade over the lamb rumps. Leave to marinate for at least 1 hour, or overnight if possible.

For the dressing

Mix the chilli with the fresh mint, white wine vinegar and extra virgin olive oil. There's no need for extra seasoning, just set the dressing aside until serving.

For the vignole

In a medium-sized saucepan, sauté the pancetta in a good glug of extra virgin olive oil and add the red onion and garlic, stirring over a medium heat until softened. To prepare the asparagus, blanch the spears in boiling salted water for 2 minutes, then remove and drop into ice cold water. Leave the tips whole and slice the stalks. Add the artichokes to the pan and stir for 2 minutes, then stir in the peas, broad beans and asparagus. Add the mint and parsley, take off the heat, and season to taste with Maldon sea salt and black pepper.

For the courgette flower

Mix the ricotta with the lemon zest, chilli flakes and chopped fresh basil, and season generously. Prepare the flowers by gently prising open the petals and removing the inner green stem. Spoon the stuffing into each flower, and press the petals back together to contain the stuffing. Make the batter just before you're ready to fry the courgette flowers. Whisk the flour and sparkling water together, and season with a generous pinch of Maldon salt and black pepper.

Heat the oven to 200°c, set the deep fat fryer to 190°c and heat a griddle pan over a high heat. Remove the lamb rumps from the marinade, and lay them in the griddle pan, colouring on each side for 3-4 minutes. Place in the preheated oven for 8-10 minutes to finish cooking, until done to your liking. Holding the courgette flowers by their trimmed stem, dip into the batter, shaking off any excess, and gently ease into the hot oil of the fryer. Fry until light golden brown, turning once, and drain on kitchen paper. The flowers can also be deep fried in a pan of hot oil, which will be at the correct temperature when a teaspoon of batter starts to sizzle when dropped in.

To serve

Reheat the vignole and remove the lamb from the oven to rest for 5 minutes. Slice each rump into six. Spoon some vignole onto each plate and top with three slices of lamb. Add the deep fried courgette flower and drizzle the lamb with the chilli and mint dressing.

Not so run of THE MILL

With slow cooked meals and a heritage spanning a millennium, Quy Mill Hotel and Spa has the culinary wisdom only time can lend.

It would be an understatement to say that Quy Mill has a long history of giving back to the community in Cambridgeshire. Earning a mention in William the Conqueror's Doomsday Book of 1086, the watermill from which Quy Mill takes its name was once integral to the village marshlands, and has kept its place at the culinary heart of the community ever since, only now the services have improved somewhat! The height of quality accommodation, dining and event experiences, Quy Mill Hotel and Spa has transformed the estate with a respectful nod to its 11th century beginnings.

More recent years have seen the addition of some luxuries to the estate, including a gym, swimming pool and spa for those visiting the estate's Health Club. Complementing these facilities are 12 acres of rolling countryside and plenty of parking for guests; only a half an hour's drive from central Cambridge, Quy Mill snuggles into the sweet spot between 'Escape to the Country' and convenient proximity to the city. With the estate boasting 51 bedrooms, 6 function rooms, car hire services, helicopter access, and day spa facilities, you'll have a hard time finding any request Quy Mill can't honour with their hallmark attention to detail.

On top of all this, the estate is home to the annual highly anticipated Cambridge Roar Festival. Now in its fourth year, Cambridge Roar is the brainchild of Tony Murdock, director of Quy Mill Hotel and Spa, where fundraising events are held between May and September to support nominated local charities. Attendees are treated to a wide range of fantastic entertainment and outstanding food and wine, as well as opportunities to bid and win exceptional prizes donated by local businesses and individuals in the event's various charity auctions. With the food a shining highlight of the festival, the catering is never less than perfect from the Quy Mill kitchen, boasting the title of only hotel in Cambridgeshire to be awarded 4 Silver Stars by the AA.

When it comes to food, Quy Mill Hotel and Spa guests are spoilt for choice all year round, with menu options ranging from beloved British classics to Irish inspired cuisine with modern twists. Guinness Beef and Oyster Mushrooms is a particular favourite of head chef Gavin Murphy, involving the patient process of slow-cooking the steak and mushrooms for 48 hours to extract every last ounce of flavour. From the Doomsday Book to this cook book, Quy Mill Hotel and Spa continues to carve its name in history one mouth-watering recipe at a time.

Quy Mill Hotel & Spa

BEETROOT SEARED SALMON WITH WARM POTATO SALAD AND SOFT BOILED QUAIL EGG

This recipe was developed by head chef Gavin Murphy and brings together some classic flavours as well as a few exciting twists that create a colourful and appetising plate of food. Happy cooking!

Preparation time: 10 minutes plus 30 minutes marinating| Cooking time: approx. 20 minutes | Serves 4

Ingredients

For the potato salad:

200g baby new potatoes

½ tsp horseradish sauce

6 tbsp mayonnaise

10g chopped chives

Salt and pepper

For the salmon:

200g salmon fillet, skin on, cut into four even-sized pieces

25g red beetroot powder

50ml olive oil

Salt and pepper

For the quail eggs:

4 quail eggs

For the garnish:

Pea shoots

Olive oil

2 tbsp tomato ketchup

Black pepper

Method

For the potato salad

Boil the potatoes in lots of salted water until tender. Drain and leave to cool a little before slicing into 5mm thick slices. Mix the horseradish sauce and mayonnaise together. Keep two tablespoons aside before adding the chives. Combine the potatoes with the dressing and season to taste.

For the salmon

Marinate the salmon for 30 minutes in the beetroot powder and 25ml of the oil, turning the fillet every 10 minutes. Place the other 25ml of olive oil in a pan and let it heat up for 1 minute. Place the salmon skin side down into the pan and allow to cook for 1 minute. Turn the salmon and let it cook for a further 2 minutes, then remove from the pan and allow to cool. Season to taste.

For the quail eggs

Place the eggs gently into a pan of boiling water and cook for a maximum of 2 and a half minutes to get runny yolks. Let the eggs cool slightly before peeling, and then set aside until serving.

To assemble

Put a tablespoon of the warm potato salad into the middle of each plate. Place a piece of salmon, skin side up, on top of the potato salad. Cut each quail egg in half and place two halves on each plate. Add a pinch of black pepper to each half. Garnish each plate with the remainder of the mayonnaise, olive oil, pea shoots and ketchup.

Have Your Cake and EAT IT

Combining the talents and passion of artisans up and down the country with their own farming expertise, Ben and Vicky have created a way of shopping online with all the convenience of a supermarket alongside all the quality and values of small independent producers.

Radmore Farm Shop started with a meeting of two minds, and has expanded to become a combination of two ways of life that make fantastic food and drink easily available across Cambridgeshire and beyond. Vicky grew up on her family's farm, Radmore, in Northamptonshire while Ben grew up in Cambridge; when the pair met they hatched a plan to bring the best of both worlds together and began by selling farm produce. The 'shed' at the gate quickly developed into a shop stocking other local suppliers' goods with an on-site butchery, and a move into Cambridge followed after many requests from city-dwellers who felt they were missing out!

It was important to Vicky and Ben that everyone could access the wonderful produce they were selling, and so creating the online store became a way to deliver to those who couldn't get to the shop on Victoria Avenue. They relaunched Radmore in 2017, allowing for a much wider range of farm produce as well as all sorts of gourmet delights from artisans up and down the country and local independents. Free-range eggs and chickens from Radmore, a plethora of higher welfare meat and poultry from Ben's butchery, freshly baked cakes and pies from Vicky's own fair hands, cheeses, charcuterie, sauces, snacks, fruit and vegetables, dairy…the list goes on because Radmore really is somewhere you can shop for everything in one go, and then have it delivered right to your door.

The aim to be so comprehensive and yet unique in the world of chain-dominated online shopping, means that Ben and Vicky often spend time discovering new people to work with who share their values. In Cambridge, Hot Numbers Coffee, Cobs Bakery, and eco-friendly BeeBee Wraps are just a few of the names linked with Radmore's. One of the newest additions to the online store's range is 'Just Add Recipe' boxes – a brainwave of Ben and Vicky's that's perfect for keen home cooks, who can discover lovely new products and use their creativity to put together delicious meals from the selection. From a cross-section of great British seasonal produce to a showcase of the best artisanal producers and suppliers out there, Radmore Farm Shop is a platform for the best food and drink to make its way easily and conveniently from source to table.

Radmore Farm Shop
VICKY'S STEAK AND ALE PIE

These are the famous pies that we have been making for the past 10 years. We use pedigree Dexter beef, because we love both the flavour and the heritage of the UK's smallest native breed. We have purposely always kept the ingredients list short, because good quality ingredients speak for themselves.

Preparation time: 30-45 minutes | Cooking time: 3-4 hours | Serves 4

Ingredients

For the filling:

15ml rapeseed oil

1 small onion, chopped

2 cloves of garlic, crushed

500ml ale (dark or light according to your preference)

450g Dexter chuck or braising steak, diced

25g plain flour

Salt and pepper, to taste

For the pastry:

100g butter, diced small

200g plain flour, plus a little extra for rolling out

Drop of cold water

1 egg, beaten

Method

For the filling

Heat the rapeseed oil in a large pan over a medium-high heat. Add the onion and caramelise, stirring often, until soft and going dark at the edges. Add the garlic and cook for a further 2 minutes. Add a drop of the ale to deglaze the pan, and give the mixture a good stir to lift any bits that are sticking to the bottom. Add the meat, and stir until it's browned all over. Add the flour and stir until well coated. Add the rest of the ale, give it a good stir to incorporate and turn the heat down to a simmer. Season well and then cover the pan and leave to simmer for 2-3 hours. Stir intermittently to prevent it sticking to the pan. When a spoon pushes easily through the meat, it's done. Leave to cool slightly and then refrigerate.

For the pastry

Rub the butter into the flour with your fingertips until it looks like fine breadcrumbs. Keep adding water a drop at a time and stirring until the mixture comes together in a ball. If it looks too wet and sticky, add a touch more flour. Turn the pastry out on to a floured surface and knead briefly until smooth. It can now be used straight away or wrapped in cling film and refrigerated until needed.

To assemble the pie

Preheat oven to 190°c and get a large deep pie dish out. Set a third of the pastry aside and then roll the bigger piece out on a floured surface until it's slightly bigger than the base of the pie dish. Line the dish with the pastry, pressing it gently to shape. Scoop the filling into the base, keeping any excess gravy if the filling has lots of sauce, and roll out the pie lid from the smaller piece of pastry. Wet the edge of the pastry base and press the lid down gently over the top to stick the edges together. Trim off the excess pastry with scissors, and snip a steam hole in the top. Brush the top generously with the beaten egg. Put the pie dish on an oven tray and bake in the centre of the oven for 30-45 minutes, until the filling is piping hot and the pastry is golden brown.

To serve

Serve straight from the oven with any remaining gravy from the pie filling, mashed potato, green veg and root veg.

Hear me ROAR

400 years of ups and downs for one of Soham's oldest pubs have been transformed into a place of warm welcomes, beautiful interiors and the tastiest food...

The Red Lion has a potted history dating back to at least 1620, and the building itself underwent a number of adaptations over the years that weren't always in its best interests. The venerable oak-framed walls ended up in danger of collapsing – held up only by a red telephone box that stands against the gable end, according to popular urban legend – when its saviours began a restoration project. Interior designer Peter Leonard bought The Red Lion in 2015, and while bringing the pub back to life he asked Lucy, a friend with a successful catering business, if she would be interested in running it. With some trepidation, Lucy agreed to get involved.

Lucy was brought up in Cambridgeshire and in the restaurant trade – her family run The Old Fire Engine House in Ely, at which she has "done every single job, starting from washing up aged 13" – so she brought a comprehensive knowledge to The Red Lion alongside, even more importantly, her own style of food that she loves to cook. The warmth and fresh flavours of Mediterranean cuisine infuse her menus both in the catering business and the pub; family holidays at their house in France and learning to cook with her dad, who travelled extensively through Europe as an archaeologist, gave Lucy the foundations to develop her relaxed and rustic dining experience.

She still does the majority of the cooking at The Red Lion, serving up daily changing dishes based around the tastiest produce sourced by local suppliers. Having recruited locally too, Lucy has a strong team who have all become part of her ethos that puts warmth and friendliness level with quality. Peter's interior matches Lucy's vision for the pub effortlessly; he has a knack for "making a space really homely" as she puts it. The merging of old and new blends her fresh, bold plates of food with the backdrop of rooms steeped in history, from the Victorian dining room to the roaring fire glowing on exposed brick and beam.

It's an all-weather destination too, helped by the lovely pub garden and a new project which will turn the adjacent coach house into an incredible events venue where Lucy plans to put on 'jazz brunches' throughout the summer. Her commitment to The Red Lion is as genuine as the food she creates there; full of love and promising a cheery welcome for years to come.

Red Lion

The Red Lion
PIGEON BREAST AND BACON SALAD WITH WALNUTS

This is one of my all-time favourite salads; it's packed full of flavour and is great as either a main or first course. It is one of the most popular dishes on our menu and people are always surprised how delicate and tender the pigeon is when cooked rare.

Preparation time: 10 | Cooking time: 10 | Serves: 4 as a main course, 8 as a starter

Ingredients

8 pigeon breasts (preferably with skin on)

Salt and pepper

75g unsalted butter

Olive oil

8 rashers streaky smoked bacon

Generous amount of mixed salad leaves

15 walnut halves, roughly broken

1 bunch of watercress

A few sprigs of flat leaf parsley, to serve

For the dressing:

1 dessert spoon Dijon mustard

50ml red wine vinegar

Salt and pepper

1 clove of garlic, crushed

50ml sunflower oil

50ml walnut oil

50ml olive oil

Method

Heat the oven to 200°c. Generously season the pigeon with salt and pepper, heat the butter and oil in a frying pan until almost smoking, and then fry the pigeon breast on a high heat until caramelised on both sides. Finish in the preheated oven for 3 minutes skin-side down in a roasting tray with the bacon. Remove from the oven and leave the pigeon and bacon to rest on a plate.

Meanwhile, make the dressing. Place the mustard in a jug or bowl and whisk with the vinegar to create the base for an emulsion. Season well with salt and pepper. Add the crushed garlic, whisk in all the oils and check the dressing for seasoning.

Toss the leaves with the dressing, but don't use all of it, just coat the leaves lightly. The remainder of the dressing can be kept in the fridge for a week.

To serve

Pile the leaves in a mound on a platter or in a large shallow bowl. Thinly slice the pigeon and scatter over the leaves along with the bacon and walnuts. Finish with watercress and flat leaf parsley.

(Twenty) Two is the magic NUMBER

In the short time since its reopening, Restaurant Twenty Two has shown Cambridge how good its local produce can be, with fine food and wine in a relaxed environment created by chef Sam Carter and partner Alex Olivier.

Sam Carter and Alex Olivier took over Restaurant Twenty Two on Cambridge's Chesterton Road at the beginning of 2018. For chef Sam, it was the realisation of a long-held ambition and for Alex it was an opportunity to change careers and begin a project they could both work on, having been kept apart by jobs in different cities. Cambridge was the perfect geographical meeting point, and the Victorian terrace was the perfect place to create an intimate dining experience that was affordable as well as high quality.

The refurbishment of the building enhanced its original features while modernising the space which had been used as a restaurant since the 1980s. Alex – who looks after front of house – transformed it with candlelit tables and timeless décor in both the main and the private dining room. "The venue really is perfect for us," she says, as it gives Sam a chance to show what he can do in a relaxed yet sophisticated setting.

His food follows much the same ethos. Having trained at Gordon Ramsay Group restaurants and Hambleton Hall in Rutland, Sam has the background to produce fine dining and the individuality to put his own spin on the concept. His dishes are developed around one main element – Yorkshire rhubarb, for example, or a cut of Dexter beef – which varies according to the best seasonal produce he can find, based on the specialised knowledge of the producers and suppliers the chef works closely with. The aim is to create food that is simple at heart, enhanced by technical cooking, and driven by great British ingredients. Whether guests choose from the à la carte, lunch, five course or seven course tasting menu, the aim is for great food and drink to be enjoyed in a welcoming environment that's appealing to everyone.

"We have already had such a mix of customers; it changes every evening," Alex says of their young but busy restaurant. With a team comprised of some old friends and some experienced hands who stayed on when Alex and Sam took over, they are "all in the adventure together," as the couple put it, and looking forward to offering more guests from Cambridgeshire and beyond their own Twenty Two experience.

Restaurant Twenty Two

35 DAY AGED DEXTER BEEF WITH WILD GARLIC RISOTTO

This is a dish that was created with nothing but seasonal ingredients in mind. Wild garlic, morels and purple sprouting broccoli are all at their best at the same time and work perfectly together. Chef's tips: wait until the last minute to add the wild garlic purée to keep it from going brown. Source the best possible meat you can as the results will be worth it!

Preparation time: 1 hour | Cooking time: 1 hour 20 minutes | Serves 4

Ingredients

For the beef:

600g 35 day aged beef sirloin

Pinch of fine salt

Drizzle of rapeseed oil

For the wild garlic purée:

300g wild garlic, picked and washed (keep the stalks)

50g butter

1 large white onion

50ml chicken stock

For the risotto:

1.2 litres chicken stock

200g Arborio risotto rice

2 small banana shallots

2 cloves of garlic

50ml dry white wine

100g Parmesan

60ml olive oil

1 lemon, juiced

50g butter

100g wild garlic purée

Salt, to taste

For the garnish:

200g purple sprouting broccoli

60g morels

For the beef sauce:

300g beef trim

4 sprigs of thyme

300g banana shallots

200g button mushrooms

100g shiitake mushrooms

Splash of vegetable oil

100g butter

2000ml beef stock

400ml red wine

Method

For the beef

Season the sirloin generously with fine salt and drizzle with a little rapeseed oil. Put the steak on to a very hot chargrill and colour each side. Roast in the oven 180°c until the meat reaches 45°c for medium, 38°c for rare and 60°c for well-done. Make sure the meat rests for about 10-15 minutes before serving.

For the wild garlic purée

Bring a pan of salted water to the boil and drop in the wild garlic leaves. Cook for 30 seconds and then refresh in iced water. Squeeze out excess water and put to one side. Melt the butter and sweat the onion until soft. When the onion is cooked, add the wild garlic stalks. Add the stock and wild garlic leaves, and then transfer the mixture to a blender. Blend until smooth and pass through a fine sieve into a chilled bowl.

For the risotto

Finely dice the shallots and garlic and begin to sweat them in the oil. When the shallot is soft and translucent add the rice. Make sure the rice is coated in the oil and then pour in the wine. Allow the wine to almost evaporate and then slowly begin to add the hot chicken stock. When the stock has evaporated add another ladleful of stock. The rice should take about 15-20 minutes to cook. Keep stirring to release the starch and avoid burning. Add the butter, Parmesan, lemon juice and finally the wild garlic purée to finish.

For the garnish

Blanch the broccoli in boiling salted water for 2 minutes or until the stem is tender but still has bite. Clean the morels thoroughly in water to make sure there is no grit. Pan fry in a knob of butter and season with salt.

For the beef sauce

Caramelise all of the beef trim with the thyme in vegetable oil and butter until nicely coloured, then set aside. In the same pan caramelise the sliced shallots and mushrooms until golden. Drain off any excess oil. Add the beef back into the pan and add the red wine. Reduce by half. Add the beef stock and reduce until the sauce is a good consistency. Keep skimming the top to remove any impurities. Add salt to taste.

To serve

Place a nice portion of the risotto in the centre of the plate. Add the garnish around the edge of the plate. Slice the beef sirloin into the required portions. Place on top of the risotto. Finally, either pour the sauce over the dish or serve it on the side.

Eat Well to
LIVE WELL

With a focus on quality, sustainable living and ethical sourcing,
Shelford Delicatessen has brought creativity and flavour to the local community.

Shelford Deli was established with a concept based on sourcing the best-tasting sustainably produced ingredients to create flavourful, wholesome food with continental influences. Charming the community from the very beginning, the team began expanding the small deli in 2010, creating a relaxed café with stone floors and a wood burner for the cold winter days, and a secluded garden with wooden benches for the summer; the perfect backdrop for serving their rustic menus.

The café menu changes seasonally, and all the food is made fresh in the deli kitchens. Breakfasts, lunches, coffee, cakes, catering and home-cooked meals showcase local favourites – including slow-roasts, cooked overnight in the wood-burning oven – with all manner of fresh salads, pestos and salsas to accompany them. What is sold in the shop is sold in the café, and chefs often nip out to the front to grab some fresh produce from the deli shelves, which could be anything from vegetables to cheese, charcuterie, pulses, wines or breads. Quality is paramount at Shelford Deli, where only the best traceable ingredients are used; the salad leaves and vibrant greens, for example, are organically grown by local company Flourish who hand plant, hand pick and use horsepower to till the earth.

Sustainability and ethically produced natural ingredients is something that the deli team take immense pride in. Their food contains no additives, preservatives or colourants, their meat is free-range, their fish is sustainably caught, and they only use suppliers that have a traceable chain. Building strong links with both local and European artisan suppliers is crucial to their ethos, and they constantly maintain these relationships by talking, visiting, planning and discussing potential products, events and ideas.

The Shelford Deli team are firm believers that where we shop, and what we eat, has a large impact on our environment and community, both locally and on a larger scale. They make that impact a positive one by providing wholesome, sustainable, good food in compostable packaging to take out, or ceramic dishes to eat in. The community is really important to the deli and its team; local custom is a mainstay of the café and its well-stocked deli shelves. Shelford Deli has at its heart a friendly community, committed people, great produce and a drive to search out the best, not just for flavour but for a healthier planet all round.

Shelford Delicatessen
TORTILLA

The three 'base ingredients' used in both of the following recipes are execllent for creating dishes that are full of flavour. They are easy to make at home, giving your dishes that extra bit of character.

Preparation time: 45 minutes | Cooking time: 1 hour | Serves: 6-8

Ingredients

Base ingredients:

For the roasted garlic paste:

3 bulbs of garlic

Olive oil

For the roasted peppers and onions:

5 peppers

5 onions

Pinch of salt

Drizzle of olive oil

For the Indian five spice:

Equal quantities of fenugreek seeds, nigella seeds, black mustard seeds, cumin seeds, fennel seeds

For the tortilla:

2 potatoes

1 white onion

2 tsp Indian five spice

8 tbsp roasted peppers and onions

9 eggs

100ml milk

⅓ tsp salt

⅓ tsp black pepper

To serve:

Free-range mayonnaise

Method

For the roasted garlic paste

Split the garlic bulbs but keep the cloves in their skins, coat in olive oil, wrap in tin foil and roast in the oven until soft. Squeeze the cloves out of their skins, add the oil from the foil, and then mash into a paste.

For the roasted peppers and onions

Thinly slice the peppers and onions, making sure the peppers are twice as thick as the onions. Spread in a single, even layer onto a baking tray, sprinkle with salt and olive oil, and roast in the oven slowly on a low heat until soft and a little caramelised.

For the Indian five spice

Dry roast the spices, then grind half of them in a pestle and mortar to release the flavours. Add to the rest of the whole seeds.

For the tortilla

Thinly slice the potatoes and onions, coat in half of the spice mix, add olive oil and salt and then either fry for roast them until they just start colouring. Mix the potatoes and onions with the prepared roasted peppers and onions.

Beat together the eggs, milk, salt, pepper, and the rest of the spice mix. Heat a non-stick frying pan and add oil. Add three quarters of the egg mixture, then turn the heat down very low. Arrange all of the potato mix in the pan with the roasted peppers and tomatoes, pushing it into the egg mix. Cook for 10-15 minutes on the lowest heat possible until there is a 1cm 'crust' forming around the edge of the pan. The middle should still be completely raw.

Take a heatproof rubber spatula or a blunt knife to scrape round the outside to prevent sticking. Place a plate on top of the pan and quickly turn both the plate and pan upside down so that the tortilla falls onto the plate. Remove the pan and place it back on the stove. Carefully slide the tortilla back into the pan to cook the other side. Tuck the edges in and cook again for 5-10 minutes, making sure it doesn't stick.

To serve

Once cooked, allow to cool. Meanwhile, make the aioli by mixing some roasted garlic paste into mayonnaise. Put a plate back on top of the pan and flip over again so the tortilla ends up on the plate. Allow to cool before cutting, and serve with aioli.

Shelford Delicatessen
DELI FIVE SPICE CHICKEN

The three 'base ingredients' that kick off this recipe are really versatile, and provide the key components of this delicious twist on roasting a chicken. The spice mix will keep in an airtight container for 4 weeks so you can add a burst of flavour to plenty of other dishes.

Preparation time: 40 minutes | Cooking time: 1 hour 40 minutes | Serves: 6-8

Ingredients

Base ingredients:

For the roasted garlic paste:

3 bulbs of garlic

Olive oil

For the roasted peppers and onions:

5 peppers

5 onions

Pinch of salt

Drizzle of olive oil

For the Indian five spice:

Equal quantities of fenugreek seeds, nigella seeds, black mustard seeds, cumin seeds, fennel seeds

For the five spice chicken:

1 free-range chicken

4 tsp Indian five spice mix

1 lemon

Salt, to taste

Olive oil

1 onion, sliced

8 tbsp roasted peppers and onions

1 tsp roasted garlic paste

Fresh mint and/or coriander, chopped

Method

For the roasted garlic paste

Split the garlic bulbs but keep the cloves in their skins, coat in olive oil, wrap in tin foil and roast in the oven until soft. Squeeze the cloves out of their skins, add the oil from the foil, and then mash into a paste.

For the roasted peppers and onions

Thinly slice the peppers and onions, making sure the peppers are twice as thick as the onions. Spread in a single, even layer onto a baking tray, sprinkle with salt and olive oil, and roast in the oven slowly on a low heat until soft and a little caramelised.

For the Indian five spice

Dry roast the spices, then grind half of them in a pestle and mortar to release the flavours. Add to the rest of the whole seeds.

For the five spice chicken

Put the whole raw chicken into a lidded ovenproof dish, and then rub half of the Indian five spice mix all over the chicken. Cut the lemon in half, putting one half inside the chicken cavity and squeezing the other half over the chicken. Sprinkle on the salt and drizzle the olive oil over the chicken. Roast covered until completely cooked. Depending on your oven, you might need to add a little water to the dish so that the juices don't dry out when cooking. Once the chicken is cooked, remove it from the pan to cool slightly. Keep all of the juices, pouring them into a measuring jug to allow the fat to separate. Carefully scoop away most of the fat and discard it.

Slice the onion finely and fry with the remaining half of the spice mix. Add all the chicken juices and some olive oil to the onions; allow to reduce for a few minutes. Turn off the heat when cooked. Pull the chicken apart, removing the bones if you wish, then mix with the prepared roasted pepper and onion. Add the roasted garlic paste to the onions and chicken juice mix and stir to combine, then mix that with the chicken and roasted vegetables.

To serve

Gently fold in the chopped herbs, and enjoy with rice or naan bread.

Getting Back to OUR ROOTS

Feeding a growing appetite for plant-based cuisine that tastes good and does good, Louise Palmer-Masterton has founded two vegan eateries in Cambridge with incredibly successful crowdfunding campaigns and long-held ambitions.

The Stem + Glory story began with owner and founder Louise's passion for healthy and delicious plant-based food and drink. Her longstanding idea of opening a vegan establishment in Cambridge developed into a pioneering crowdfunded business that saw over £100,000 raised in just 21 days, culminating in Stem + Glory's first opening in October 2016. The restaurant on Chesterton Road took off straight away, winning hearts and minds with its internationally-inspired menu. As a concept, it aims to contribute to the burgeoning movement towards eating more ethically and showcase just how irresistible vegan alternatives can be when it comes to eating out.

Just over a year later, the Stem + Glory brand branched out to include a café in the city centre. The King Street location has a vibrant atmosphere, speedy service and a wide range of options for take-away or eat-in lunches plus breakfast on weekdays and brunch over the weekends. Already looking towards the future, Louise is planning to set up another Stem + Glory eatery, this time in London. After a third hugely successful crowdfunding campaign, reaching her target in just six hours, she plans to combine the best of the restaurant and café to begin a national roll out of her increasingly popular concept.

The food and drink itself is at the heart of Stem + Glory's success. From the signature kimchi pancakes to the protein-packed smoothies, everything is 100% plant-based and freshly made in each of the on-site kitchens. Cakes, hot and cold drinks, raw snacks, indulgent meals and on-the-go lunches offer everyone the opportunity to get a taste of the alternative options that contribute to more ethical and healthier lifestyles for everyone. It helps that they taste amazing and are created by a team of talented chefs, of course! Both premises are also fully licensed so can offer vegan wines and craft beers, and for those who want to embark on a real journey of discovery into the cutting edge of plant-based cuisine, fine dining evenings at Stem + Glory – featuring a seven course tasting menu – are unmissable, sell-out events.

Louise's ambitions have brought a refreshing new option for eating out to Cambridge. From its unconventional but very fruitful beginnings, Stem + Glory continues towards its aim of contributing to a more peaceful and harmonious world, full of plant-based cuisine that's too good to resist.

Stem + Glory

Stem + Glory

BLUEBERRY + BANANA 'CHEESECAKE'

At Stem + Glory our raw desserts are an absolute winner, and one of our best sellers. Cashew nuts are a really versatile ingredient; once soaked and blended they make the most deliciously creamy desserts. We vary our cheesecake according to the seasons, and you can easily adapt this yourself, substituting the blueberry and banana for raspberries, cocoa or even just lemon and vanilla.

Preparation time: 1 hour plus chilling or freezing time | Makes 12 portions

Ingredients

For the base:

110g cashews (can also use almonds)

100g desiccated coconut

265g pitted dates

30g coconut oil, melted

2½g vanilla powder (or extract)

60ml water

5g cocoa powder

For the filling:

720g cashews

220g maple syrup

100ml lemon juice

220g coconut oil (melted)

90ml water

5g vanilla powder (or extract)

Pinch sea salt

110g blueberries (frozen)

1 banana

12½g blueberry powder

15g soy lecithin

Method

For the base

Soak the cashews (or almonds) in water for 15 minutes. Drain and discard the water. Add the cashews (or almonds) and all the remaining ingredients to a food processor and pulse until a sticky, crumbly mixture is made. Line a 25cm springform tin with baking paper. Transfer the mixture into the tin and flatten the base evenly. Press down well and smooth over using the back of a spoon.

For the filling

Soak the cashews in hot water for 15 minutes. Drain and discard the water. Add the cashews and all the remaining ingredients except the lecithin to a blender and blend until a smooth and viscous liquid has formed. If your blender is low powered, this may take 10 minutes or more. Thoroughly stir the lecithin into the liquid, and then pour the filling over the base. Leave the cheesecake in the fridge to set, or freeze and then leave it out for an hour to defrost before serving.

To serve

We serve ours with some blueberry compote and slices of caramelised banana. You can also serve it with fresh blueberries, or just eat it straight from the fridge!

Stem + Glory
NORI ROLLS

Stem + Glory founder Louise has been experimenting with plant-based foods for more than 30 years, and loves clean and healthy Japanese cuisine. It's incredibly easy to 'veganise' many Japanese recipes, and these Nori rolls are a firm favourite at Stem + Glory Chesterton Road. You can use different crunchy vegetables if you prefer, and they also work well without noodles. This recipe uses tofu, but at Stem + Glory we use marinated tempeh too, if you have that to hand.

Preparation time: 30 minutes | Serves: 6

Ingredients

For the wasabi mayonnaise dip:

1 block of silken tofu

1 lime, zest and juice

½ tsp salt

½ tbsp vinegar

1-2 tsp wasabi according to taste

For the marinated tofu:

1 block of firm tofu

40g tomato purée

½ tsp (or to taste) cayenne pepper

1 tsp smoked paprika

1 tsp salt

40g sunflower oil

For the noodles:

1 pack of fine rice noodles

2 tbsp sesame oil

For the vegetables:

1 large carrot

1 red pepper

1 cucumber

100g white or red cabbage

1 baby gem or any soft leaf lettuce

1 pack nori sheets

Method

First, make the dip. Blend all the ingredients until the mixture is super smooth. Add more wasabi according to your preference.

Next, cut the firm tofu into long square strips, approximately 1cm thick. Mix the remaining ingredients together to make a marinade, add the tofu and leave to marinate for 10 minutes. Bake the coated tofu in the oven for 10-15 minutes.

Add the sesame oil and rice noodles to boiling water and cook or stand according to the instructions on the packet. Stir to avoid the noodles clumping. Drain and rinse the noodles with cold water to quickly stop the cooking process.

Peel the carrots. Thinly slice the red pepper, cucumber and carrot to 5cm in length and 2cm in thickness. Slice the cabbage and lettuce in to fine strips on their side, to preserve the 'wavy' shape.

Dampen a clean cloth slightly and then place the nori paper on top. Moisten slightly, and then place a handful of Rice Noodles, 3 batons of Red Pepper, 3 batons of Cucumber, a large pinch of Cabbage, the same of lettuce and two pieces of Tofu on a quarter of the sheet closest to you. To roll, fold the edge closest to you over the filling and tuck it under, then roll that over the remaining nori paper. To stick the ends down, wet the edge and press firmly.

To serve

Slice the roll into four pieces at a diagonal, and serve with the wasabi dip.

A Living HISTORY

Nestled in the countryside that surrounds Bartlow, The Three Hills aims to give something back to the Cambridgeshire community.

Located in the heart of the pretty village of Bartlow, The Three Hills was bought by Chris and Sarah Field who wanted to do something for the community. About to move to the village themselves, the couple wanted to create a place that was appealing to both locals and visitors, and give people "the warmest welcome in Cambridgeshire". After a long planning process, the couple were finally able to begin restoring the pub to its former glory as a traditional village pub. A seventeenth century Grade II listed building, The Three Hills was originally opened as an alehouse in 1847, and is the only pub in the close-knit village.

The pub has become the hub of the community, with villagers holding Parish Council meetings there and enjoying discounted drinks in the cosy library room. Chris and Sarah want their pub to feel welcome to everyone, and they offer six lovingly-refurbished bedrooms for those travelling from afar to visit the local area. Just walking distance from The Three Hills are the largest Roman barrows in England, and the pub itself is named after these three huge Roman burial mounds.

The couple actively employ local staff, so that they are always on-hand to offer information about the area and nearby walking routes. The whole team aspire to provide excellent service; The Three Hills always aims to go that extra mile to make customers feel welcome. The chef, Keith, has been at The Three Hills from the very beginning, and has been awarded two AA Rosettes for his food.

By offering two menus, The Three Hills has something for whatever mood you're in. The bar menu is more hearty and traditional, with dishes like fish and chips, homemade Scotch eggs, and mac and cheese, and the dinner menu consists of more classic, stylish food, such as their wild mushroom risotto and côte de boeuf. You can eat from either menu wherever you are in the building, whether that's next to the cosy log burners, in the oak-beamed dining room or in the new landscaped garden, where a pizza oven is soon to be built. Brought back to life by Chris and Sarah, The Three Hills offers a vibrant place where anyone can feel at home.

The Three Hills

ROAST GUINEA FOWL WITH SMOKED BACON AND BLACK GARLIC

You can prepare the guinea fowl legs the day before
so the bonbons are ready to cook just before serving.

Preparation time: 30 minutes, plus chilling time | Cooking time: approx. 3 hours | Serves 4

Ingredients

For the guinea fowl:

2 guinea fowl breasts, skin on

2 guinea fowl legs

200g goose fat

1 bay leaf

2 cloves of garlic

Plain flour

1 egg, beaten

Breadcrumbs

For the sauce:

2 shallots, diced

1 carrot, diced

1 stick of celery, diced

1 bay leaf

500ml chicken stock

100ml white wine

50g redcurrant jelly

For the black garlic purée:

20g shallot, finely chopped

25g black garlic

100ml chicken stock

5g soft brown sugar

For the garnish:

4 rashers smoked streaky bacon

4 asparagus spears

100g fresh garden peas

100g broad beans

Knob of butter

A handful of pea shoots

Method

For the confit legs

Place the legs into a baking tray with the goose fat, bay leaf and garlic. Season with salt and pepper and then cook the legs for 2½-3 hours in the oven at 150°c. When the meat is nearly falling away, take out and leave to cool then drain off the excess fat. Strip the meat from the bone; discard any skin, bones and sinew to leave just the picked meat. Once cool (not cold) start to shape the meat into ping pong sized balls. Put the bonbons in the fridge to chill. When completely cold, roll each bonbon in flour, then dip in egg, and then coat with breadcrumbs. Set aside while you prepare the rest of the dish.

For the sauce

Sweat the diced vegetables and bay leaf in a pan for 5 minutes. Add the white wine and reduce by half, then add the redcurrant jelly and chicken stock. Reduce the liquid by two thirds or until it reaches sauce consistency. Set aside until ready to serve.

For the black garlic purée

First soften the shallots, then add the rest of the ingredients and bring up to the boil. Remove the pan from the heat and then place the contents in a blender and blend until you have a smooth purée.

Roasting the guinea fowl

Season the guinea fowl breasts with salt and pepper and then place them skin side down in a hot pan with a little oil. Leave for 1-2 minutes until the skin is golden brown, then turn and leave for 1 minute. Place in the oven for 7-10 minutes at 200°c.

For the garnish

Place the streaky bacon in between two sheets of parchment paper and then two baking trays, keeping the bacon flat, and place in the oven until the bacon is crisp. Trim the asparagus and then drop the spears into boiling salted water with the peas and beans. Simmer for 2-3 minutes and then drain when tender. Toss the vegetables in a hot pan with butter, and then fry the guinea fowl bonbons in a deep fat fryer for 3 minutes at 180°c.

To plate

Place the garlic purée in a plastic squeeze bottle and starting from the middle of the plate, draw concentric circles of increasing size until you have about four radiating out from the centre. Slice the guinea fowl into three pieces per breast and place them randomly onto the purée along with the bonbons. Break the bacon into shards and lean against the guinea fowl. Spoon over the peas and beans, and add the asparagus. Finally, pour some of the sauce over all the ingredients and garnish the dish with pea shoots.

Word on the STREET

Indian street food that comes to you in the great tradition of Mumbai's tiffin wallahs – what more could you want for a working lunch or relaxed meal out?

Having established the fine dining restaurant Navadhanya in Cambridge, owners and cousins Arun and Krishna were drawn to the idea of bringing the same authentic flavours to more people in a more affordable and casual setting. Tiffin Truck is not actually a truck, but a restaurant based on the concept of Indian street food. There is a huge variety of freshly cooked snacks and on-the-go meals across the subcontinent, from masala dosa in the south to Indo-Chinese sweet and sticky paneer.

Arun and Krishna are from the south of India themselves, and have travelled throughout the country as well as working in London as distributors for Indian ingredients. Their desire to bring the lunchbox culture of India to Cambridge dates back to the days of the Raj, when British afternoon tea replaced the local Indian practice of taking a light meal at that hour. Every weekday in Mumbai, where the tiffin tradition began, you can still see hundreds of tiffin wallahs racing around the streets with their bicycles piled high with stainless steel tiered boxes, delivering hot lunches to workers.

Tiffin Truck offers the same speedy delivery service if you can't get to the restaurant, and you can even collect your takeaway in a traditional stainless steel lunchbox – not only stylish but reusable for the restaurant – for a small deposit. Your meal could include nibbles such as bhel, a crunchy puffed rice with Bombay mix, a bite of deep fried spiced chicken, and naza or bun tikki (that's Indian pizza or burger) to name just a few of the options! The different menu sections provide the perfect mix-and-match option for any time of day between 11 and 11, when food is served at the restaurant, and can be enjoyed with a cocktail or Indian craft beer on the side.

For exciting lunches (to beat any boring sandwich eaten at your desk by miles) or laid-back evenings, the eclectic menu and colourful interior recreate the atmosphere of an Indian bazaar in Cambridge. The vibrant and rustic feel of Tiffin Truck is combined with an uncompromising approach to quality ingredients and a great dining experience for everyone. Students can pop in just as easily as the office workers with whom the concept is so popular; Tiffin Truck is a cheerful fusion of Indian market favourites and convenience with all of the flavour.

Tiffin Truck
MEEN POLICHATHU (ROASTED FISH WRAPPED IN BANANA LEAF)

This dish is very famous in the southern part of India, where it's considered a local delicacy and is generally prepared with freshwater fish. We use salmon fillet, marinated with various spices and a punchy ground paste, cooked in banana leaf to retain all the moisture and layers of flavour.

Preparation time: 30 minutes, plus overnight soaking | Cooking time: 1 hour | Serves: 2

Ingredients

For the salmon:

2 small onions

2 green chillies

¼ tsp ginger paste

¼ tsp garlic paste

10g mustard

1 tsp chilli power

Pinch of turmeric powder

180-200g salmon fillet

1 sprig of curry leaves

2 lemon leaves

1 banana leaf, large enough to cover fish completely

For the sauce:

100g small onions

¼ tsp ginger paste

3 green chillies

Pinch of turmeric powder

1 tsp chilli powder

100ml coconut milk

Pinch of salt

For the lentil pancake:

100g green moong dal

1 tsp cumin seeds

100g boiled rice

Pinch of salt

1 sprig of curry leaves

Method

For the salmon

Sauté the onion, chillies, ginger and garlic pastes, mustard, turmeric, chilli powder, curry leaves and lemon leaves in oil. Leave this mixture to cool and then cover the salmon fillet with it. Wrap the fish in the banana leaf and fry it on a tawa (or a frying pan) over a medium heat, or it can be cooked in oven at 180°c.

For the sauce

Heat two tablespoons of oil in a pan and sauté the chopped onion, ginger and green chillies until golden brown. Add the turmeric and chilli powder and continue to sauté the mixture until the spices are toasted. Add the coconut milk, 500ml of water and salt, mix well to make a sauce and boil to reach a good consistency.

For the lentil pancake

Soak the green moong lentils overnight and then blend them with the cumin seeds and boiled rice. Incorporate the salt and curry leaves, and then make a small round pancake with the mix. Cook it for 5 minutes or until the pancake turns light brown.

To serve

Serve the meen polichathu by first placing a lentil pancake on the plate, layering fish over that and then topping everything with the curry sauce. You can add a bowl of plain rice which goes well as a side dish.

Four SEASONS

Tom Dolby takes a unique approach to baking in his small-batch artisan bakery, using Cambridge's bounty to the best of its potential by focusing on seasonal cakes, savoury bites and treats.

Established in 1998, Tom's Cakes is an artisan craft bakery with a unique focus on seasonality. With provenance at the heart of what they do, many of their ingredients are sourced from local farms and suppliers. From Uncle Howard's apples in Bluntisham to Alpha Farm's free-range eggs in Hilton, their supply chain rarely stretches further afield than fifty miles. It is this home-grown, hand-made approach to their baking that has made Tom's Cakes a favourite on the Cambridgeshire food scene over the last twenty years.

Coming from a long line of bakers, Tom Dolby is the Tom in Tom's Cakes. His mother's family opened their first bakery shop in 1803 but Tom decided at a young age that he wanted to branch out on his own and take a different approach to baking. Influenced by artisan bakers in the UK and his travels in New Zealand and Australia, Tom wanted to create a product where everything could be made from scratch, in small batches, using simple staple ingredients, fruit and vegetables that were available seasonally. It is this approach that has driven the development of the bakery's repertoire, from lavender cake in the summer to apple and cinnamon cake in the autumn. The team strive constantly to add new goodies to the counter to tempt their customers!

Originally retailing through farmers' markets in East Anglia and London, Tom and his business partner Ian decided to open their first shop in St Ives in 2014. The shop enjoys a prime location in the busy market town and being a former Victorian market toll house has a unique appeal. It proved such a hit with the locals that Tom and Ian decided to pull away from the markets side of the business and focus on developing a second shop, this time in Cambridge.

Based on bustling Mill Road, Tom's Cakes bring a distinctly British baking flavour to the cosmopolitan Cambridge independent food scene. With plenty of seating inside and a garden to enjoy on warmer days, the Cambridge branch provides a relaxing pit-stop for residents and tourists alike. It's not just about the cakes either; the range of savoury options – including panini, quiche, salad, snacks and soup – makes Tom's a great breakfast and lunch spot too, as well as the ideal place to satisfy that sweet tooth with a little special something away from the norm.

Tom's Cakes
ROSEMARY, LEMON AND OLIVE OIL CAKE

We are always on the lookout for interesting, new recipes and were first introduced to this cake as a dessert at a friend's dinner party. We decided to adapt it to be a gluten-free addition to our range and it's now a popular, regular feature on our counters.

Preparation time: 20-30 minutes | Baking time: 40 minutes | Serves 6-8

Ingredients

For the cake:

40g plain gluten-free flour

90g ground almonds

145g caster sugar

1 tsp gluten-free baking powder

4 free-range eggs

200ml olive oil

10g fresh rosemary, chopped

1 unwaxed lemon, zested

For the icing:

½ unwaxed lemon, juiced and zested

100-200g icing sugar

Method

For the cake

Combine the gluten-free plain flour, ground almonds, caster sugar and gluten-free baking powder in a mixing bowl. Crack the eggs into a jug and beat them together. Slowly add the eggs and oil to the mixing bowl, stirring continuously into the dry ingredients to make a batter. Add the chopped rosemary and lemon zest and stir.

Grease and line an 8 inch round cake tin. Pour the cake batter into the prepared tin. Bake in a preheated oven at 160°c for 20 minutes, turn the tin and bake for a further 15-20 minutes. Your cake should be golden and the surface should spring back when pressed lightly. Allow to cool on a rack.

For the icing

Put the juice and zest of the lemon into a bowl. Add enough icing sugar to make a thin, watery paste. Drizzle the icing over the top of the cake and spread using a palette knife. Decorate with a light sprinkling of rosemary and lemon zest.

To serve

This cake is delicious on its own but works equally well as a dessert, served with raspberries and crème fraîche.

A Loaf STORY

White Cottage Bakery and Baking School is home to award-winning baker, Helen Underwood, a passionate advocate of local provenance, who shares her passion with keen and would-be bakers through her inspiring workshops.

Nestled in a picturesque Cambridgeshire village, White Cottage Bakery has made a name for itself producing locally sourced, hand-crafted sourdough loaves. The little farmhouse is more than just an award-winning micro-bakery, though – it is also home to regular bread-making workshops, where budding bakers can hone their skills under head baker Helen's instruction. Artisan bread is Helen's passion: she founded the bakery because she believes everybody should be able to get their hands on delicious, freshly-baked and additive-free loaves.

It's a recipe for success that starts with simplicity – flour, water, salt, yeast and a little practice! So it's easy to see why she's equally passionate about passing on her expertise, offering a wide range of workshops. Helen has a host of Great Taste awards and accolades from the World Bread Awards under her belt – most recently two Golds in 2017 – and teaches all the workshops herself. From introductory classes for the uninitiated to specialty sourdough or sweet dough courses, there's something for everyone. With a maximum of eight people, each class is small enough to ensure that everyone gets the time and attention they need.

Helen's mission statement is simple: everyone should go home with a bag full of hand-made bakes, a full stomach (breakfast and lunch feature delicious fresh food alongside bakery favourites), a new set of skills and a smile on their face. "There's always a lovely positive energy about the whole thing," says Helen, who loves seeing new and familiar faces at the workshops and helping them hone their craft so they can produce really great bread in their own homes.

Her midweek 'How to make the perfect...' workshops are a newer addition, offering shorter classes on how to produce brioche burger bun, babka, and more besides. Whatever she's baking – or teaching – Helen emphasises the importance of using fresh, high quality and locally sourced ingredients. Her recipes feature herbs from her own cottage garden, wild garlic picked in the nearby woods when in season, fruits from her village orchard and grain grown down the road at Wimpole Estate and ground at nearby Fosters Mill.

Helen believes that great bread should be at the heart of the community, and by supporting traditional local businesses and helping to minimise 'food miles' everyone can feel great about eating it in more ways than one!

White Cottage Bakery
POTTED CHEESE

This recipe is a firm favourite with our workshop students, who, by lunchtime, have usually worked up quite an appetite. We love to serve a jar of this potted cheese alongside our seasonal salads, bread and charcuterie. You'll find it's a great way to use up the remains of a dinner party cheese board, and it only improves in flavour if kept in the fridge for a few days.

Preparation time: 10 minutes | Serves 8-10

Ingredients

250g quark

250g mixed cheeses (6-8 varieties of cheeses made up of whatever you have to hand, avoiding blue cheese or rinded soft cheese)

½ tbsp fresh thyme leaves

Zest of ¼ lemon

Pinch of chilli flakes

2 tbsp extra virgin olive oil

1 handful fresh mixed herbs, chopped

Cheese inspiration:

Good mature cheddar (especially quartz varieties)

Mature red Leicester

Cheshire

Gouda

Wensleydale

Grana Padano

Comté

Manchego

Gruyère

Emmental

Soft goats cheese (the rindless, spreadable kind)

Feta

Parmigiano Reggiano

Pecorino

Method

Take a large bowl and, crumbling or grating where appropriate, add each of the cheeses to the quark. Zest about ¼ of a lemon into the mixture, and combine with the chopped fresh thyme and a pinch of chilli flakes (more if you're feeling daring!). Mix well. Taste at this stage to make sure you have a good balance of flavours – if too salty, add more mild cheese; if it's not salty enough, a little more Italian hard cheese or feta should do the trick.

Transfer to a preserving jar, such as a Kilner jar, and press down. Cover with a couple of tablespoons of fresh mixed herbs of your choice, such as flat leaf parsley, oregano, marjoram, mint, chives or coriander. Finally, pour over a couple of tablespoons of good quality extra virgin olive oil and seal.

Best if made 48 hours before needed, as this allows the flavour to develop. Keep refrigerated for about a week.

The DIRECTORY

These great businesses have supported the making of this book; please support and enjoy them.

The Anchor
63 North Street
Burwell
Cambridge
CB25 0BA
Telephone: 01638 743970
Website: www.theanchorburwell.net
Family and dog-friendly 18th-century village inn serving seasonal British food and good wine.

The Baking Jin
Email: thebakingjin@gmail.com
Telephone: 01223 911178
Website: www.thebakingjin.com
Facebook, Instagram and Twitter:
@thebakingjin
Oriental inspired, baked in Cambridge.

Balkan Pottery
Telephone: 07977 548316
Website: www.balkanpottery.com
Email: info@balkanpottery.com
Rustic and robust pottery for cooking and serving fuss-free, delicious food and drink.

Bedouin
98-100 Mill Road
Cambridge
CB12BD
Telephone: 01223 367660
Website:
www.bedouin-Cambridge.com
Traditional North African cuisine with home-style tagine cooking in a real Bedouin tent!

Al Casbah
62 Mill Road
Cambridge
CB12AS
Telephone: 01223 561666
/ 01223 579500
Website: www.al-casbah.com
Algerian charcoal BBQ, meze and tagines.

Bedouin Caterers
Email: Info@bedouincaterers.com
Telephone: 01223 245714
North African and Algerian catering available for events including weddings and private parties taking the best of the two restaurants and bringing it to your occasion.

Cambridge Blue Belles WI
Website:
www.cambridgebluebelleswi.co.uk
Facebook: CamBlueBelles
Twitter: @CamBlueBellesWI
Instagram: cambluebelleswi
Cambridge Blue Belles is a fun and friendly WI group meeting in the heart of Cambridge. Our members range from 20 to 50, and are bon vivants, freelancers, professionals, students, scientists, artists, knitters, bakers... often all at the same time!

Bohemia St Neots
16 Cross Keys Mews
Market Square
St Neots
Cambridgeshire
PE19 2AR
Telephone: 01480 716265
Website: www.bohemiastneots.com
By day, a modern British bistro and coffee shop serving freshly made seasonal, local food and seriously good coffee. By night, a cosy restaurant serving tapas and cocktails in a vibrant and stylish environment.

Bridges Cambridge
20 Bridge Street
Cambridge
CB2 1UF
Telephone: 01223 300800
Website: www.bridgescambridge.co.uk
Bright and welcoming café focusing on healthy and modern cuisine with an oriental twist, serving fresh juices, breakfast, lunch and afternoon tea and offering catering.

Burwash Larder
New Road
Barton
Cambridge
CB23 7EY
01223 264600
www.burwashlarder.com
Farm shop and deli on the outskirts of Cambridge. We grow our own asparagus and rear rare breed pigs.

Bury Lane Farm Shop
A10 Bypass
Melbourn
Royston
SG8 6DF
Telephone: 01763 260418
Website: www.burylanefarmshop.co.uk
Bury Lane Farm Shop offers a friendly atmosphere brought to you by a family-run team. The focus on local producers gives you a unique shopping experience.

Cambridge Food Tour
Telephone: 01223 269 991
Tour website:
www.cambridgefoodtour.com
Events website:
www.foodanddrink.events

Cambridge Market
Market Square
Cambridge
CB2 3QJ
Telephone: 01223 457000
Website:
www.cambridge.gov.uk/markets
Award-winning general market with 100 stalls offering a fabulous range of local produce and international street food, seven days a week.

The Cambridge Organic Food Co.
7 Penn Farm Studios
Harston Road
Haslingfield
Cambridge
CB23 1JZ
Telephone: 01223 873300
Website: www.cofco.co.uk
Delivering boxes of locally grown organic fruit and vegetables to homes and businesses in Cambridge and the surrounding area.

Chocolat Chocolat
21 St Andrew's Street
Grand Arcade
Cambridge
CB2 3AX
Telephone: 01223 778982
Website: www.chocolatchocolat.co.uk
Award-winning independent chocolate shop, famous for its handmade Belgian chocolate bouquets, handmade ice cream and hot chocolate shots.

Chris Mann
BBC Radio Cambridgeshire
Twitter: @chrismannbbc
Email: chris.mann@bbc.co.uk

Country Kitchen
21 Church Street
Haslingfield
Cambridge
CB231JE
Telephone: 01223 874284
Purveyors of Cambridgeshire produce, gifts and homeware, hampers, and delicious homemade food to take away.

The Cambridge Distillery
20-22 High Street
Grantchester
Cambridge
CB3 9NF
Phone: 01223 751146, ext. 3
Website:
www.cambridgedistillery.co.uk
The Cambridge Distillery is an internationally-recognised multi-award-winning business, named three consecutive times as the most innovative distillery in the world.

The Cambridge Gin Laboratory
10 Green Street
Cambridge
CB2 3JU
Telephone: 01223 751146, ext. 1
Website: www.cambridgeginlab.co.uk
The Cambridge Gin Laboratory is an interactive space in the centre of Cambridge, dedicated to the appreciation of gin.

Dog in a Doublet
Northbank
Thorney
Peterbough
PE6 0FH
Telephone: 01733 202256
Website: www.doginad.co.uk
Dog in a Doublet is a family-run gastro farmhouse with rooms, set on the river Nene in the heart of the Fens.

Dulcedo Patisserie
60 Hills Road
CB2 1LA
Cambridge
Telephone: 01223 364 111
Website: www.dulcedopatisserie.co.uk
Modern, innovative patisserie with fresh pastries, petit gateaux, chocolate treats and events catering for the sweet-toothed and curious of Cambridge.

Elder Street Cafe & Deli
Debden Barns
Elder Street
Saffron Walden
CB11 3JY
Telephone: 01799 543 598
Website: www.elderstreetcafedeli.co.uk
Purveyors of homemade and locally sourced produce.

The Geographer
103 Station Road
Impington
Cambridge
CB24 9NP
Telephone: 01223 233228
Independent, family-run cafe, deli and gift shop situated in the pretty twin villages of Histon and Impington just north of Cambridge.

The Gog Farm Shop
Heath Farm
Shelford Bottom
Cambridge
CB22 3AD
Telephone: 01223 248352
Website: www.thegog.com
Family-owned and award-winning farm shop, deli, café and butchery bringing the best of local food and drink to Cambridge.

Hot Numbers Coffee
Unit 6 Dales Brewery
Gwydir Street
Cambridge
CB1 2LJ
Telephone: 01223 359966
4 Trumpington Street
Cambridge
CB2 1QA
Telephone: 01223 300730
Website: www.hotnumberscoffee.co.uk
Speciality coffee roasters with two cafes in the heart of Cambridge. Proper coffee, exciting seasonal brunch menu, friendly staff, live jazz and real piano!

Jack's Gelato
6 Bene't Street
Cambridge
CB23QN
Website: www.jacksgelato.com
Gelato and sorbet made by hand in the Italian style but with British flavours, using the very best ingredients, all produced sustainably and ethically by Jack and his small team.

Johnsons of Old Hurst
Church Street
Old Hurst
Huntingdon
Cambridgeshire
PE28 3AF
Telephone: 01487 824658
Website:
www.johnsonsofoldhurst.co.uk
Extensive butchers and farm shop, tea room and steak house, all set on a working farm which supplies the majority of the meat sold on site.

Little Acre Kitchen
7 Crown Street
St Ives
Cambridgeshire
PE27 5EB
Telephone: 01480 300597
Website: www.littleacrekitchen.co.uk
Community-friendly café serving brunch and lunch dishes made with fresh, local ingredients.

Mark Poynton
Twitter @markjpoynton
Instagram @markjpoynton
Website: www.mjprestaurant.com
Chef-patron of Michelin-starred Cambridge restaurant Alimentum between 2012 and 2017. Mark's first solo cook book will be out in 2019 and a new restaurant in Cambridge will be opening in 2018.

The Mermaid in Ellington
High Street
Ellington
PE28 0AB
Telephone: 01480 891106
Website:
www.themermaidellington.co.uk
Family-run restaurant nestled in the heart of the Cambridgeshire countryside, with a true passion for the food they offer on an ever-evolving menu, using innovative techniques to create a fine dining experience in a relaxed atmosphere.

Midsummer House
Midsummer Common
Cambridge
CB4 1HA
Telephone: 01223 369299
Website: www.midsummerhouse.co.uk
Two Michelin-starred restaurant by Daniel Clifford and head chef Mark Abbott, with tasting and à la carte menus.

Navadhanya
73 Newmarket Road
Cambridge
CB5 8EG
Telephone: 01223 655399
Website: www.navadhanya.co.uk
Restaurant showcasing the art of Indian fine dining, featured in the Michelin Guide 2018.

The Oak Bistro
6 Lensfield Road
Cambridge
CB2 1EG
Telephone: 01223 323361
Website: www.theoakbistro.co.uk
Classic bistro situated in an iconic former coaching inn with an eclectic wine list and internationally inspired, locally sourced food. Find us on Facebook @ TheOakBistroCambridge.

The Olive Grove
100 Regent Street
Cambridge
CB2 1DP
Telephone: 01223 778575
Website: www.the-olivegrove.co.uk
Family-run restaurant serving modern Greek cuisine.

OliveOlive
Olive Tree Cottage
School Road
Broughton
Huntingdon
Cambridgeshire
PE28 3AT
Telephone: 07824387933
Website: www.oliveolive.co.uk
Extra-virgin olive oils direct from our family farm, and authentic 'village-style' halloumi cheese handmade the traditional way in Cyprus.

Parker's Tavern
Regent Street
Cambridge
CB2 1AD
Telephone: 01223 606266
Website: www.parkerstavern.com
Launching in 2018, Parker's Tavern will be a destination restaurant and bar serving good, honest, locally sourced food – a delicious taste of Cambridge, overseen by chef Tristan Welch.

Pint Shop
10 Peas Hill
Cambridge
CB2 3PP
Telephone: 01223 352293
Website: www.pintshop.co.uk
Beer house inspired by the best of traditional British food and drink including over 100 gins, a range of local brews, bar snacks and classic dishes with a twist.

Prana Indian Restaurant
97 Mill Road
Cambridge
CB1 2AW
Telephone: 01223 229988
Website: www.pranarestaurant.co.uk
Modern Indian cuisine drawing on family history and innovation to create fresh food and an atmospheric dining experience.

Prevost

11 Priestgate
Peterborough
PE1 1JA
Telephone: 01733 355912
Website:
www.prevostpeterborough.co.uk
Small family-run restaurant serving modern British food with great cocktails and an interesting wine menu.

Provenance Kitchen

Telephone: 07779304833
Website: www.provenancekitchen.com
Wood-fired catering bringing restaurant quality food to all occasions.

Puddini

Tasting Room and Kitchen
16 Berrycroft
Willingham
Cambridgeshire
CB24 5JX
Telephone: 01954 263028
Website: www.puddini.co.uk
Unique catering for corporate events, weddings, private parties and intimate gatherings.

Quy Mill Hotel & Spa

Church Road
Stow-cum-Quy
Cambridge
CB25 9AF
Telephone: 01223 293383
Website: www.cambridgequymill.co.uk
A stylish AA 4 silver starred hotel full of character and charm.

Radmore Farm Shop

Website: www.radmorefarmshop.co.uk
Online supermarket, delivering the best produce from Radmore farm and other local and independent artisan producers directly to your door.

The Red Lion

17 High Street
Soham
Ely
Cambridgeshire
CB7 5HA
Telephone: 01353 771633
Website: www.redlionsoham.com
17th century pub, beautifully renovated and serving freshly cooked food with Mediterranean influences in a relaxed and welcoming setting.

Restaurant Twenty Two

22 Chesterton Road
Cambridge
CB4 3AX
Telephone: 01223 351880
Website: www.restaurant22.co.uk
Modern British dining room offering delicious food in a relaxed environment.

Shelford Delicatessen

8 Woollards Lane
Great Shelford
Cambridge
CB22 5LZ
Telephone: 01223 846129
Website: www.shelforddeli.co.uk
Kitchen, deli and café which prides itself on quality, sustainably produced ingredients, and offers rustic handmade food to either eat in, take out or order for an event.

Stem + Glory Restaurant

121 Chesterton Road
Cambridge
CB4 3AT
Telephone: 01223 324575

Stem + Glory Café

13 King Street
Cambridge
CB1 1LH
Telephone: 01223 314331
Website: www.stemandglory.uk
Plant-based eateries in Cambridge offering table service lunch and dinner at the Chesterton Road location, and breakfast, brunch and lunch at King Street.

The Three Hills Bartlow

Dean Road
Bartlow
Cambridge CB21 4PW
Telephone: 01223 890500
Website: www.thethreehills.co.uk
Traditional 17th century village inn with award-winning restaurant, five star accommodation, cosy log fires and outside dining. Children and dogs always welcome.

The Tiffin Truck

22 Regent Street
Cambridge
CB2 1DB
Telephone: 01223 366111
Website: www.thetiffintruck.co.uk
A fast and funky bar and restaurant where you can enjoy Indian market food dishes alongside Indian craft beers and cocktails.

Tom's Cakes

32 Mill Road
Cambridge
CB1 2AD
19 Market Hill
St Ives Cambridgeshire
PE27 5AL
Telephone: 01487 842200
Website: www.tomscakes.co.uk
Artisan craft bakery and shop with a unique focus on seasonality.

Restaurant Twenty Two

22 Chesterton Road
Cambridge
CB4 3AX
Telephone: 01223 351880
Website: www.restaurant22.co.uk
Modern British dining room offering delicious food in a relaxed environment.

White Cottage Bakery and Baking School

Carey Hill
Church Lane
Kingston
Cambridge
CB23 2NG
Telephone: 01223 264557
Website: www.whitecottagebakery.com
An award-winning farmhouse bakery, running bread making workshops throughout the year.

Other titles in the 'Get Stuck In' series

Lakes & Cumbria features Simon Rogan's L'Enclume, Forest Side, Hawkshead Relish, Fyne Fish, L'al Churrasco, Cartmel Cheeses and lots more.
978-1-910863-30-5

The Nottingham Cook Book 2 features Bakehouse, Welbeck Estate, Memsaab, Sauce Shop, Starkey's Fruit, 200 Degrees Coffee, Homeboys, Rustic Crust and lots more.
978-1-910863-27-5

The Devon Cook Book sponsored by Food & Drink Devon features Simon Hulstone of The Elephant, Noel Corston, Riverford Field Kitchen & much more.
978-1-910863-24-4

The South London Cook Book features Jose Pizarro, Adam Byatt, The Alma, Piccalilli Caff, Canopy Beer, Inkspot Brewery and lots more.
978-1-910863-27-5

The Brighton & Sussex Cook Book features Steven Edwards, The Bluebird Tea Co, Isaac At, Real Patisserie, Sussex Produce Co, and lots more.
978-1-910863-22-0

The Liverpool Cook Book features Burnt Truffle, The Art School, Fraîche, Villaggio Cucina and many more.
978-1-910863-15-2

The Bristol Cook Book features Dean Edwards, Lido, Clifton Sausage, The Ox, and wines from Corks of Cotham plus lots more.
978-1-910863-14-5

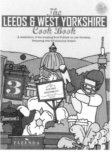

The Leeds Cook Book features The Boxtree, Crafthouse, Stockdales of Yorkshire and lots more.
978-1-910863-18-3

The Cotswolds Cook Book features David Everitt-Matthias of Champignon Sauvage, Prithvi, Chef's Dozen and lots more.
978-0-9928981-9-9

The Shropshire Cook Book features Chris Burt of The Peach Tree, Old Downton Lodge, Shrewsbury Market, CSons and lots more.
978-1-910863-32-9

The Norfolk Cook Book features Richard Bainbridge, Morston Hall, The Duck Inn and lots more.
978-1-910863-01-5

The Lincolnshire Cook Book features Colin McGurran of Winteringham Fields, TV chef Rachel Green, San Pietro and lots more.
978-1-910863-05-3

The Essex Cook Book features Thomas Leatherbarrow, The Anchor Riverside, Great Garnetts, Deersbrook Farm, Mayfield Bakery and lots more.
978-1-910863-25-1

The Cheshire Cook Book features Simon Radley of The Chester Grosvenor, The Chef's Table, Great North Pie Co., Harthill Cookery School and lots more.
978-1-910863-07-7

The Oxfordshire Cook Book features Mike North of The Nut Tree Inn, Sudbury House, Jacobs Inn, The Muddy Duck and lots more.
978-1-910863-08-4

All books in this series are available from Waterstones, Amazon and independent bookshops.

FIND OUT MORE ABOUT US AT WWW.MEZEPUBLISHING.CO.UK